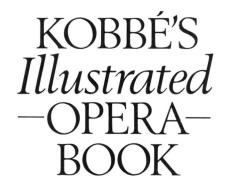

KOBBÉ'S
Illustrated
—OPERA—
BOOK

KOBBÉ'S
Illustrated
—OPERA—
BOOK

Twenty~six of the World's
Best~loved Operas

The Earl of Harewood, 1923–

George Henry Hubert Lascelles!!!

G. P. Putnam's Sons

New York

To my grandchildren, Sophie, Emily, Rowan, Ben, Orly,
Tanit, Eddy, Tom, Ellen, Tewa and Amy – not forgetting
Poppy and Sam.

If they get even half as much pleasure from opera as I have,
it will have been worthwhile.

G. P. Putnam's Sons
Publishers Since 1838
200 Madison Avenue
New York, NY 10016

Designed and produced by
Bellew Publishing Company Ltd
7 Southampton Place WC1A 2DR

Library of Congress Cataloging-in-Publication Data

Harewood, George Henry Hubert Lascelles, Earl of, 1923-
Kobbé's illustrated opera book: twenty six of the world's best-loved operas by
the Earl of Harewood.
160 p. 26.3 cm.
Bibliography: p.
Includes index.
1. Operas – Stories, plots, etc. 2. Opera. I. Kobbé, Gustav, 1857-1918. II. Title.
MT95.H2 1989
782. 1'026'9 – dc20

1 2 3 4 5 6 7 8 9 10

ISBN: 0-399-13475-1

Printed in Spain by Graficas Estella, S.A.

Frontispiece: *Maria Ewing as Rosina in the second
scene of Rossini's* Il barbiere di Siviglia *at Glyndebourne
in 1981. The opera was designed by William Dudley and
produced by John Cox.*

ACKNOWLEDGEMENTS

Special thanks go to Simon Bainbridge for all his help and inspiration.

The Publishers and author also wish to thank the following for permission to
reproduce photographs:

Catherine Ashmore pp. 27, 128, 140; Simon Bainbridge Collection pp. 46,
48, 56, 58, 124; Clive Barda pp. 38-9, 49, 50, 61, 63, 68, 69, 71, 85, 87, 90,
91, 111, 115, 139, 143, 155; The British Library p. 31; Zoë Dominic pp. 32,
33; Guy Gravett/Picture Index, frontispiece, pp. 12, 16, 19, 40, 43, 44, 149,
150, 152; Lord Harewood pp. 23, 90, 133; Marina Henderson Gallery
p. 138; Houston Rogers/Theatre Museum pp. 125, 154; Angus McBean
p. 22; Andrew March p. 37; Opera Magazine pp. 57, 75, 144, 145;
Royal Opera House archive pp. 102, 104; Donald Southern p. 81;
John Starr/Entertainment Corporation pp. 103, 106; Stuart-Liff Collection
pp. 7, 8, 9, 10, 11, 20, 21, 25, 36, 42, 53, 60, 66, 73, 78, 84, 89, 96, 97, 100,
101, 108, 112, 114, 120, 121, 125, 132, 136, 148; John Vere Brown p. 85:
Reg Wilson p. 40; Woodmansterne Picture Library pp. 14, 15, 26, 27, 34, 54
55, 78, 82, 95, 104, 107, 119, 127, 131, 134.

Contents

Foreword

In operatic history hardly a decade has ever passed without the howl going up: 'Opera is finished'. Yet in spite of being dubbed élitist by those who do not like it, out of date by those who cannot write it, and boring by those who have never heard it, opera seems to have become *more* popular in the 1970s and 1980s rather than *less*. Certainly, it counts for more in several countries which have come to it a little later than Italy, where it was invented; or Germany, where it took on intellectual respectability; or France, where it became for the family in the nineteenth century almost what television is in the twentieth. It flourishes, for instance, in the United States of America and in the United Kingdom, and it may well come to do so in Australia and Canada as well.

One of opera's great attributes is that it can mean almost anything to anyone who is prepared to allow theatre or music (preferably both together) to speak to them. It used to be the major vehicle for dramatic spectacle until that role was usurped by cinema. It has been, almost since it was invented, the happy hunting ground of those who delight in the sound of the human voice and its various accomplishments. It can give almost unsurpassed pleasure to the devotee of musical architecture on a grand scale – think of *The Ring* or *Don Carlos* – or it can satisfy the fantasies of the weariest of post-prandial hedonists – think of Puccini. It can delight with its wit and what it conceals beneath the smoothest of surfaces, or it can terrify with the ferocity of its passion – think of

The blonde Maria Jeritza was claimed to be Puccini's favourite Tosca. She epitomised the prima donna of legend – wilful, tempestuous and a good singer.

Così fan tutte and *Otello*. It can comment on the human condition and the pleasures and miseries of those who inhabit it, like *Le nozze di Figaro* or *La traviata,* or it can preach various kinds of morality, like *Die Zauberflöte* or Pfitzner's *Palestrina*. It can summon up saints like Beethoven's Leonore or Tchaikovsky's Tatiana; sinners like Mozart's Don Giovanni and Britten's Peter Grimes; monsters like Pizarro and Scarpia; or people made wise through suffering, such as the Marschallin, Mimi or Madam Butterfly. And there is somebody to identify with each of them.

We talk about Mozart's *Don Giovanni*, not da Ponte's, and Verdi's *La traviata*, not Piave's, but of course the librettist has a hand in it all as well as the composer. Sometimes they are one and the same – Wagner with his legends and his literary

Mattia Battistini, the most famous late nineteenth-century bel canto baritone, as Don Giovanni.

convolutions, or Leoncavallo with his dramatising of a case of murder tried by his magistrate-father. Sometimes the librettist is not much more than a literary hack, who has, however, a thorough knowledge of composer and audience, like Piave with Verdi or Schikaneder with Mozart. Sometimes the libretto is taken from an existing play which needs little adaptation, like *Figaro, Il barbiere di Siviglia* or *Yevgeny Onyegin*. At other times the librettist is a considerable and original literary figure, like Hofmannsthal, Boito, da Ponte or Ira Gershwin. Sometimes regular practice is reversed: instead of the composer setting what the librettist has written, the librettist (like a translator) has to invent phrases to fit what has already been composed. Even Verdi was not immune from such cart-before-the-horse behaviour.

Whatever the aims, whatever the methods, in the end the only thing that matters is the resultant opera and its effect on the public. Some are obviously hard to bring off, like *Tristan und Isolde*, which has little action, much metaphysical argument and title roles built for titans; or *Boris Godounov*, which can seem dramatically disconnected; or even *Don Giovanni*, which promises the earth and seldom quite delivers. Some virtually never fail, like *La Bohème, Traviata* or *Figaro*. Others in performance almost invariably bring disappointment in a major role: like *Carmen*, where composer and librettist have hit the nail firmly on the head, but raised expectations unreasonably high.

Opera not only aims at something basic to human needs and aspirations, but is, by its nature and history, essentially a popular form. Let us take aspirations first. From earliest times and through every kind of means – rain dances, Greek drama and the Christian mass, as well as the earliest specific attempts at opera (the Camerata in Florence, a band of aristocrats who tried to recreate Greek drama at a stroke, with everything set to music) – civilised man has conveyed drama through music. Whether we were dancing to impress the elements or to seek intercession, or were using music to enhance our highly sophisticated efforts at achieving catharsis, or are conducting ritualised worship of a God who denies us the adoration of a graven image, or even when we are singing nursery rhymes to our children (what about 'Pop goes the weasel'?), we have been close to *dramma per musica* and have been pioneers of the art of opera, some of whose early examples had specifically this title. Even the English, who were suspicious of opera as a foreign form, invented the Masque, which used hardly less music but carried on the drama in spoken word as opposed to sung.

All this contributed to something which rapidly became popular and was never thought of, still less condemned, as élitist. This is odd, in a way. Not where rain dancing, Greek drama or the mass were concerned, for they were certainly not confined to a particular group. But the Camerata in Florence was not searching for dramatic truth through a newly-minted medium, but aiming at a piece of high-brow reconstruction. Opera was lucky in that within decades of its 'invention' (if one can use so crude a word) it had found its first genius, Claudio Monteverdi, and that, whether he wrote for the court in Mantua (as with *Orfeo*) or for the public theatre in Venice (*L'Incoronazione di Poppea*), he spent his time consciously or unconsciously laying down principles which, however much developed and added to since, have never been superseded.

Within thirty years of Monteverdi's *Orfeo* (1607), public theatres for operatic performance were being built in Venice and operas written for them in some quantity – 350 by the end of the seventeenth century. Adulation of the prima donna was on its way, so that by the time opera arrived in England, to be sung by Italians in their native language to audiences which did not understand it, Dr. Johnson felt obliged to describe the *Italian* opera (*not*, be it noted, opera in general) as an 'exotic and irrational entertainment'. And who, in the linguistic circumstances, shall attempt to say him nay?

None the less, for most if its history, opera has been a popular form, appealing to what in Elizabethan England were described as 'groundlings' just as much as Shakespeare did, with his rhetoric and his processions, his high-flown passions and his barely suppressed violence. Substitute arias and vocal flights for 'rhetoric' and you might be describing opera in the eighteenth and nineteenth centuries. You would find *Il matrimonio segreto* encored in its entirety on its first night;

Carmen, notoriously unsuccessful at its première, clocking up 35 performances within three months; and La Scala's records showing that, in their first runs, *Così fan tutte* was given 39 performances, *Don Giovanni* 40, even *Otello* as many as 25 and *Falstaff* only two fewer. Many lesser works, some unheard of today but plainly in demand then, were scheduled for between 25 and 50 performances at La Scala over 100 years ago. In the twentieth century, Menotti's double bill of *The Telephone* and *The Medium* and later his even more successful *The Consul* were put on for Broadway runs in New York, *The Consul* in its initial stage appearance. Four cycles of *The Ring* were scheduled and filled at Bayreuth in 1976, the centenary year, and in the same year English National Opera completed no fewer than seven cycles of the mighty work – three

Lauritz Melchior as Tristan: a massive voice at the service of a singer of great intensity.

The original Carmen, Célestine Galli-Marié.

in London, four on tour – and all in the language of the audience. Not even Beethoven's Fifth Symphony or Tchaikovsky's First Piano Concerto are scheduled for runs quite like this, but it is not abnormal for opera. If the singers could stand the strain, probably more performances of some of these giant works would be scheduled – in which context it may be salutary to remember that at La Scala in 1887 the same Otello, Desdemona and Iago, according to the records, appeared on all 25 evenings.

*

What keeps the operatic *aficionado* coming year after year? Is it love of the music, or of the drama, or of that combination of the two which is uniquely opera? Is it a fascination for voice, for singing, for comparing one interpretation with another? Or a compulsion to see what each new production or cast can do to shed new light on a work sometimes too well known? For most of us, more than one of these factors. Great singers can change public perception of an opera or a whole era of operatic history – think of Callas and the operas of the Italian *ottocento* – and conductors and producers can provide revelations even in the pivotal works of the repertory which you had assumed to be done to death. Always there is the evening to hope for when the combination is just right – the single voice easily performs the miracle of dominating the 100-piece orchestra, the imagination takes off and music and drama combine in the unique amalgam of opera.

In the final analysis, the true fascination of opera does not lie in a display of virtuosity or in the pleasure of comparison, not even in discovering treasure trove where only dross was expected. It lies within music itself – its ability to reveal and connect, the speed with which it can pin down aspects of character, skewer attempts at evasion, suggest what lurks beneath the surface, contradict the ostensible truth and replace it with something much more worrying, the way it can disarm and overwhelm. When as a schoolboy I first read Kobbé, I was intrigued by a description of Gluck's attempts to fill his music with drama and by a reference to a passage in *Iphigénie en Tauride*. 'In the second act', Kobbé wrote, 'while Orestes is singing "Le calme rentre dans mon coeur", the orchestral accompaniment continues to express the agitation of his thoughts. During the rehearsal the members of the orchestra, not understanding the passage, came to a stop. "Go on all the same", cried Gluck. "He lies. He has killed his mother".' At the time, I ached to hear the passage in question and was not disappointed ten years later when I first got the chance.

There is, I fear, no opera by Gluck among these twenty-six, so the question, 'Are these truly the twenty-six most popular operas?', is perfectly valid. Are they the 'best'? Or your (more probably my) favourites? The answer must, I suppose, be 'yes' and 'no' to all these questions. Can the twenty-six most popular exclude *Faust*, or the twenty-six best omit *The Ring* or *Wozzeck*? Can *I* leave out half-a-dozen of my own first choices? I was determined not to be bound by statistics, but equally determined to take account of popular taste and bring in the twentieth century without flouting the choices of most opera-goers. I felt there had to be another Russian opera beside *Boris* and at least one representative of Czech, English and American schools – though whether *Porgy and Bess* is representative of anything except itself and Gershwin is debatable, just as it is whether one should include Janáček in preference to Smetana (or indeed Dvořák), or *Peter Grimes* rather than *Billy Budd* or *The Turn of the Screw* – or Tippett's *The Midsummer Marriage*, for that matter. And is *Jenůfa* more representative than *Katya Kabanova*, which I believe is the greater work?

Choice is not easy, though it has also not been unenjoyable to exercise. Nor is there ultimately a 'correct' or a 'true' choice, in itself 'better' than the one I have, not without consultation, eventually made. I have tried to put each work in some kind of historical context; give a synopsis of the story so that those who know it already will be reminded of their way about and others may see a glimmer of relevance as they read; and above all, suggest what the composer has been attempting in this work – where he has best succeeded, where he has pioneered or trodden old ground more effectively than others before him, what he has left enduringly behind and what someone meeting one of these operas for the first time may expect to find. I have also tried to show why a particular work became popular in the first place and why its popularity has been maintained or increased over the intervening years.

If this musing gives pleasure to those who have already dipped their toes in operatic water and not found the temperature hostile, that is a cause for satisfaction. Better still, if it persuades a waverer to take the plunge, then a new recruit may have been

The Marschallin in Der Rosenkavalier *became Lotte Lehmann's most successful role.*

gained for that great army which believes that the human race's instinct to make drama through music is a strong one. To be described as recruiting sergeant for such an army – to borrow a phrase my publisher told me was included in the review of another book – is surely the highest praise we can hope for.

Elena Rizzieri (Susanna) and Sena Jurinac (the Countess) at Glyndebourne in 1955.

WOLFGANG AMADEUS MOZART

Le nozze di Figaro

The Marriage of Figaro

Opera buffa in four acts by Mozart; text by Lorenzo da Ponte, after Beaumarchais. Mozart seems to have been well on with his new opera by November 1785 and to have finished the overture, which he always wrote last, on April 29, 1786. The première was in Vienna on May 1, 1786 with Mmes Laschi, Storace, Bussani and Gottlieb and Messrs Mandini, Benucci and Kelly, directed by Mozart himself.

CHARACTERS

Count Almaviva	Baritone
Figaro, *his valet*	Baritone
Doctor Bartolo, *once the Countess's guardian*	Bass
Don Basilio, *a music-master*	Tenor
Cherubino, *a page*	Soprano
Antonio, *a gardener*	Bass
Don Curzio, *a lawyer*	Tenor
Countess Almaviva	Soprano
Susanna, *her personal maid, engaged to Figaro*	Soprano
Marcellina, *formerly the Countess's duenna and now her housekeeper*	Soprano
Barbarina, *Antonio's niece*	Soprano

Time: Eighteenth century
Place: The Count's château of Aguas Frescas, near Seville
Approx Act Lengths: Act I 45 min., Act II 50 min., Act III 42 min., Act IV 35 min.(without Marcellina and Don Basilio arias)

Although *Die Entführung aus dem Serail* (1782) was a big success in Vienna, and a blow apparently struck for Mozart's dream of a flourishing German opera, it became apparent that the court still favoured exclusively Italian opera and the Italian singers who put it over with such brilliance: Mozart was reduced to writing additional numbers for other composers' works (quite a common practice in those days). Following an abortive attempt at a specially written Italian libretto, Mozart fell in with another Italian, Lorenzo da Ponte, who was in favour with the Emperor Joseph II and believed he could persuade him to allow Beaumarchais's daring (and in Vienna still proscribed) comic play, *Le Mariage de Figaro,* as an opera.

Beaumarchais's *Le Mariage de Figaro,* a sequel to the distinctly less adventurous *Le Barbier de Séville,* was finished in 1778, but it was, with some reason in view of the subversive subject, forbidden the stage: it was not performed until 1784. Da Ponte judged the Emperor's mood right and the ban on *Figaro* was lifted for opera. One may think this decision enlightened, but it is none the less curious; for it was not so much individual lines or incidents which caused concern in Paris and other capitals, but the whole subject, with servants plotting against their masters, and not only showing them in a bad light (which produced more hilarity than protest among the French ruling classes), but actually prevailing in the intrigues which are the stuff of both play and opera.

No doubt it was da Ponte and his prospective libretto which the Emperor was judging and not Mozart, but when in the last finale the moment comes for the Count finally to beg forgiveness – after massive and very public misbehaviour – Mozart writes phrases of such nobility and beauty that to deny the Count pardon would have required a stony-heartedness quite beyond either the sprightly Rosina of *Le Barbier* or the maturer and sadder lady she becomes in *Le Mariage*. We must take care not to credit the Emperor with preternatural foresight nor to anticipate events, even though it immediately postulates one of opera's most powerful weapons, the ability of music in a single phrase to touch the heart and make connections with previous events which have also been encapsulated in music – to suggest, in short, incomparably well what goes on beneath the surface.

The opera's action takes place within a single day (Beaumarchais's subtitle is *La Folle Journée*).

Act I.   Figaro's plan to marry Susanna is under threat from Marcellina, who, aided by Doctor Bartolo, means to compel him either to repay a debt or in default marry her. Meanwhile, Susanna rejects the room the Count has assigned to her and Figaro (because convenient proximity to the Countess also makes for easy access by the Count), discomfits Marcellina and consoles a disconsolate Cherubino, who has been sacked for flirting (aria: 'Non sò più cosa son', I know not what I am), before fending off the attentions of the Count. When Basilio comes in, both the Count and Cherubino are in hiding, but the former emerges to complain about Basilio's gossip, while the latter is flushed out soon after. Cherubino witnessed the Count's advances towards Susanna and is banished to the Count's regiment; the act ends as Figaro speeds Cherubino on his way (aria: 'Non più andrai', No more games).

Act II.   The Countess (aria: 'Porgi amor', Grant, O love) hears Susanna and Figaro plan an assignation for Susanna and the Count, who will also get an anonymous letter saying the Countess has a secret rendezvous. Cherubino will impersonate Susanna and the Count, caught red-handed, will have to stop his philandering. Cherubino (aria: Voi che sapete')

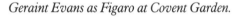

Geraint Evans as Figaro at Covent Garden.

The Count (Robert Kerns) gives Susanna (Ileana Cotrubas) a veil.

is being measured for his part when he panics at the sound of the Count's voice outside and hides. The finale finds the suspicious Count in a towering rage, but when to everyone's surprise Susanna emerges from Cherubino's hiding-place, he begs forgiveness. However, even Figaro's quick-wittedness is taxed when the Count first quizzes him about the anonymous letter and then cross-questions him about a paper dropped by whoever jumped from the dressing-room window (it was Cherubino, but Figaro maintains it was he). The act ends with his position heavily under siege as Marcellina, Bartolo and Basilio lodge formal complaints against him for breach of promise.

Act III. The Count now feels secure enough to arrange an assignation with Susanna (duet: 'Crudel, perchè finora', Cruel one, why so long make me languish?), but explodes with indignation when he overhears her and Figaro in blatant intrigue against him (aria: 'Vedrò, mentr' io sospiro', I shall see, while I am sighing). The plot's twists continue and no sooner has the Count given judgement for Marcellina than it is convincingly shown she is Figaro's mother (sextet). The Countess (aria: 'Dove sono', Where are they now) dictates the letter Susanna is to send to the Count (duet: 'Sull' aria', I am ready) and, as Susanna slips it to him during the wedding celebrations (Fandango), he pricks his finger on the pin used to seal it.

Act IV. In the garden, Barbarina bewails the loss of the pin she must return to Susanna and enlists the help of Figaro, who begins to fear the worst and for a time loses his way in the comedy of mistaken identity (aria: 'Aprite un po' quegli occhi', Open a

Frederica von Stade (Cherubino) and Ileana Cotrubas (Susanna) at Glyndebourne in 1973.

Elizabeth Harwood (the Countess) and Ileana Cotrubas (Susanna): Glyndebourne, 1973.

little your eyes). Susanna changes clothes with the Countess and sings ostensibly to a lover, knowing all the time that Figaro is eavesdropping (aria: 'Deh, vieni non tardar', Now come, do not delay). Cherubino flirts with someone he believes to be Susanna (in reality the Countess), the Count pays court to his own disguised wife, the bamboozled Figaro fulminates. Suddenly, he rumbles Susanna's disguise and laughs at her indignation when he makes up to her, then joins her in wooing so extravagant that the Count falls for the ruse and summons witnesses to testify to his wife's infidelity. All supplications for forgiveness are turned down until the Countess's voice joins the others and a happy ending is in sight.

Like *Don Giovanni, Così* and *Barbiere,* of the operas discussed in this collection, *Le nozze di Figaro*

is composed in orchestrally accompanied numbers, solo or concerted, which serve to crystallise dramatic situations; these numbers are separated by recitative accompanied only by keyboard and a single stringed instrument – commonly called *recitativo secco* – which serve to push the story along. The audience needs the information the recitatives provide and the essence of opera is the heightened comment the composer with the help of his librettist can make in the sections of developed music. Mozart above any composer of the eighteenth century evolved a musico-dramatic skill to combine the two functions of imparting dramatic information and commenting on it: the finales of *Figaro*'s second and fourth acts provide perhaps the greatest examples of this ability in the operatic literature of any century.

Figaro shows Mozart working at the height of his

powers. The characterisation is superb, whether of the neglected but still high-spirited Countess, with her two great arias; or the skittery page Cherubino, who is young enough to be allowed liberties and old enough to take advantage of them[1] and has two immortal songs, 'Non sò più cosa son' and 'Voi che sapete'; or the formidable figure of the Count, too busy and energetic to have time for an aria before the third act, but revealing, when it comes, a feudal personality far from comic. As early as the first act's trio, modern opinion would describe the Count's and Basilio's treatment of Susanna as sexual harassment.

The drama's female protagonist, Susanna, is among opera's longest feminine roles and is, like Pamina in *Die Zauberflöte*, one of the finest examples of Mozart's attempt to show in music an ideal feminine figure – lively, as full of fun as of depth, loving, above all loyal – and none of Mozart's other heroines gets a more purely musical aria than the last act's 'Deh, vieni non tardar', when she is simultaneously arch-romantic and super-tease. It is interesting that in so masculine a century it is the male who loses touch in the last act and the female who dominates it – again, like Pamina. Her masculine opposite number epitomises a certain kind of Latin hero – macho, quick-witted, tough, amusing, not just resourceful but a man of feeling as well. Perhaps that is how Mozart saw himself, but I doubt whether his Figaro is anything like as much of a self-portrait as the Figaro of *Le Barbier* is of Beaumarchais.

1. In the third of Beaumarchais's plays, *La Mère Coupable* (The Guilty Mother), Cherubino fathers the Countess's child!

Mozart above everything understood the shadows beneath the surface, the banana-skins waiting for even the most confident to slip on. *Figaro* is full of examples. The second act's finale has them in plenty: the Count's storming of his wife's dressing-room only to see Susanna step coolly from the closet – an operatic moment no-one who knows the opera can fail to look forward to; or Figaro's relish when he and his two female supporters remember that the page's commission was unsigned and he can hurl the Count's snare in his face. In Act IV, Figaro's aria of protest against the wiles of women and the unfairness of his own situation has the recitative begin in a mood of revenge, but ends on a note of something not far from comedy as he comes near to joining the horns in the orchestra in mockery of the eternal and very Latin comic figure of the cuckold.

The last finale has always seemed to me one of the ultimate operatic achievements. Pushing comedy to extremes, the dark tapestry is shot through with flashes of illumination and the night is full of thunder until, as if after a storm, it all clears – once Susanna understands Figaro saw through her disguise and was in fact not making up to the Countess in all seriousness but to his own wife in pure fun. Figaro's little B-flat tune arrives to prove to us that the happy ending, which might in another context be little more than the halfway house of convention, is, for Figaro and Susanna, the real thing.

Mozart's skill is unrivalled, but it went a great deal further than writing dextrous, well-shaped ensembles and arias. With it he would constantly penetrate the workings of the human heart and comment with an acuteness and a humanity matched by no other composer.

WOLFGANG AMADEUS MOZART

Don Giovanni

Dramma giocoso in two acts by Mozart, text by Lorenzo da Ponte. The première was in Prague on October 29, 1787, with some of the same singers as the previous year's *Figaro*, including in the title role the 22-year-old Luigi Bassi, who had earlier sung the Count; Teresa Saporiti (Donna Anna), Caterina Micelli (Donna Elvira), Catarina Bondini (Zerlina), Antonio Baglioni (Don Ottavio), Felice Ponziani (Leporello) and Giuseppe Lolli (Masetto and Commendatore) made up the cast. In Vienna the opera was presented a year later with Francesco Albertarelli as Don Giovanni , Aloysia Lange (Donna Anna), Catarina Cavalieri (Donna Elvira), Morella (Don Ottavio) and Benucci (Leporello).

CHARACTERS

The Commendatore	Bass
Donna Anna, *his daughter*	Soprano
Don Ottavio, *her betrothed*	Tenor
Don Giovanni, *a young nobleman*	Baritone
Leporello, *his servant*	Bass
Donna Elvira, *a lady of Burgos*	Soprano
Zerlina, *a country girl*	Soprano
Masetto, *betrothed to Zerlina*	Baritone

Time: Seventeenth century
Place: Seville
Approx Act Lengths: Act I 85 min., Act II 81 min.

After the great success of *Le nozze di Figaro* in Prague in the winter of 1786, it was natural for Mozart to be invited to write a new opera for this important second city of the Austro-Hungarian empire and natural for him to turn again to da Ponte. The text for the new work, written against time, drew on Bertati's libretto for Giuseppe Gazzaniga's opera of the same name and da Ponte may even have enlisted the help of other professional writers, including (rumour has it) the adventurer Casanova. When the opera was presented in Vienna a year later, Donna Anna was sung by Mozart's sister-in-law Aloysia Lange, with whom he had once (to his father's chagrin) been in love, but who had rejected him; and Donna Elvira was sung by the celebrated Catarina Cavalieri (an Austrian in spite of her name), who was the mistress of his rival, the Italian composer Salieri, and for whom Mozart wrote frequently. For her he composed a new aria, 'Mi tradì', just as for the tenor he substituted 'Dalla sua pace' for 'Il mio tesoro', the tenor preferring not to sing the latter, possibly because he could not.

This is perhaps the moment to point to one of *Don Giovanni*'s problems: it is too full of arias, many of them famous, for its own dramatic good. Perhaps it is a problem with most eighteenth-century opera. Singers demanded them, the public expected them; and of course the aria, like all developed music, is a potent operatic weapon, the moment for the composer to comment in depth on the drama he has

Leporello's Catalogue aria (Glyndebourne, 1982): Richard Van Allan, with Elizabeth Pruett (Elvira).

set going. But almost inevitably arias hold up the action in a way it is sometimes hard to defend, because you feel it was the singer who wanted it so. Don Ottavio's 'Il mio tesoro' is a chastely flowing melody often thought of as the touchstone of a tenor's ability in classical song: his 'Dalla sua pace' and Donna Anna's 'Non mi dir' are not far behind it. Each provides a magnificent opportunity for a singer, but you need not be a dry-as-dust commentator to ask how valid is their comment in context and how much they can ever contribute to the drama. Quite different are Zerlina's 'Batti, batti', by the end of whose ingratiating melodies Masetto has willingly succumbed to his sweetheart's wiles, or Donna Anna's 'Or sai chi l'onore', which erupts as an

implacable call for justice. For the rest, if they constitute an offence against the dramatic flow, one could argue that Mozart commits it with such grace and invention that the listener must accept advice offered in quite different circumstances: when something is inevitable, all you can do is lie back and enjoy it − which is what audiences, while pundits fume, have been doing for generations.

Mozart enjoyed in opera swinging between comedy and high seriousness, striking a balance few other composers attempted, much less brought off. This tendency reached its apogee in *Don Giovanni*, whose overture foreshadows what will follow in an *andante* looking forward to the solemnity of the Commendatore and the supper scene and an *allegro*

Luigi Bassi, the original Don Giovanni, sings the Serenade.

suggesting the more serious side of the eponymous hero.

Act I. Leporello keeps watch (aria: 'Notte e giorno faticar', Night and day I'm kept on guard) while a masked Don Giovanni attempts the seduction of Donna Anna, whose father breaks in on the scene and is killed by the would-be seducer. Donna Anna's fiancé, Don Ottavio, is left to comfort her.

Don Giovanni attempts to make up to Donna Elvira, not realising at first that he has met her before, but leaves Leporello to divert her attention with a catalogue of his master's conquests (aria: 'Madamina, il catalogo è questo', My lady, this is the catalogue).

Peasants are celebrating the engagement of Zerlina and Masetto, the former of whom takes Don Giovanni's fancy (duet: 'Là ci darem la mano', You'll put your hand in mine). Donna Elvira interrupts them, leads Zerlina away and then returns to disrupt a conversation between Don Giovanni, Donna Anna and Don Ottavio, at the end of which Donna Anna is convinced she has found her father's murderer (aria: 'Or sai chi l'onore', Know now who stole my honour). Don Ottavio is determined to help her (aria: 'Dalla sua pace', On her peace of mind).

Don Giovanni gives a party (aria: 'Finch' han dal vino', Let wine be flowing) at which Zerlina ingratiates herself with Masetto (aria: 'Batti, batti, o bel Masetto', Beat me, beat me, my fine Masetto). As the finale begins, Don Giovanni leads Zerlina and Masetto to his house. Anna and Ottavio, who have Elvira with them, are invited by Leporello to join the party (minuet: Trio of the masks) and as three different dances are in progress inside, Don Giovanni attempts the seduction of Zerlina and is denounced as reprobate and murderer.

Act II. In lively mood, Don Giovanni and Leporello change clothes to mock the sentimentally inclined Donna Elvira before Don Giovanni serenades her maid (aria: 'Deh, vieni alla finestra', Come to the window, my treasure). He diverts a lynching party brought against him by Masetto and gives a severe beating to its leader, who is consoled by Zerlina (aria: 'Vedrai, carino', You'll see, my darling).

Meanwhile, Leporello is leading away Donna Elvira, whom he has tricked into thinking that he is Don Giovanni. They are waylaid by Donna Anna and Zerlina and their respective partners, who threaten Leporello's life (sextet): he contrives to escape (aria: 'Ah, pietà! Signori miei!', Ah, have pity, my lords). There follow the principal arias for Don Ottavio ('Il mio tesoro', Speak to my treasure) and Donna Elvira ('Mi tradì, He betrayed me) before we return to the drama to find Don Giovanni and Leporello meeting fortuitously in the cemetery where the Commendatore is buried. His commemorative statue comes to life and accepts Don Giovanni's mocking invitation to supper. After Donna Anna's aria ('Non mi dir', Do not tell me) the finale ushers in a brilliant if solitary supper for Don Giovanni: his meal is interrupted by the Commendatore's statue, which drags him away to

Virgilio Lazzari (Leporello) and Ezio Pinza (Don Giovanni) in the pre-war Salzburg production.

hell and damnation. A moralistic epilogue for the remaining characters brings the opera to the conclusion traditional for dramatic representations of the Don Juan legend.

Mozart and da Ponte called *Don Giovanni* a *dramma giocoso*, but some of their joint practice belies the description, much of the action and music being ambitiously serious in character. Often Don Giovanni himself, aided and abetted by Leporello, tips the balance back towards some aspect of comedy, either by the brilliance of his recitative, the mocking character of the action, or by the melodic playfulness of his contribution to the set pieces. Nowhere is this ambiguity more evident than in the trio early in Act II. Donna Elvira voices her melancholy in a tune of exquisite beauty, but her reward is for her heartless lover to change clothes

with his servant (in order later to woo her maid) and, while Leporello mimes his master, mock her himself with exaggerated protestations of love. Taken wholly seriously, as Donna Elvira's music suggests, a charge of callousness could be levelled at composer and librettist. But if the performance has established a convention of ambivalence, Mozart's unique blend of comedy and pathos can be appreciated in all its subtlety. The question remains: can what is unbearable if taken seriously be tolerable as comedy?

It has often been remarked that Don Giovanni is put forward as the great seducer – at the start of the opera Leporello lists 2,065 conquests – but, during the action and starting with Donna Anna, he fails consistently with every attempt he makes (if one can afford to ignore the analysts who maintain that

Donna Anna's implacable drive for revenge is caused by his success with her *before* the curtain rises and not by her father's death at all). This may demonstrate a weakness of construction, but nobody with ears to hear can miss the essential quality of sexual charisma in the music the opera's hero has to sing, either as he remarks on 'L'odor di femmina' just before Donna Elvira's entry or as he makes up to Zerlina before and during 'Là ci darem la mano' or as he serenades Donna Elvira's maid in one of Mozart's most beguiling numbers.

The tone of the opera, then, comes considerably from the almost frenzied brilliance of Don Giovanni's recitative and the exuberant sexuality of something like his 'Finch' han dal vino', but no-one on that account should fail to appreciate that the score's serious side is on a level wholly sublime. Early on, the trio in F minor for Giovanni, Leporello and the dying Commendatore propounds what we might call its metaphysical aspect, reinforced when the Commendatore reappears as a statue, and to the sound of a deep voice is added the solemnity of trombones (used only when the statue is on the stage). It is at its most serene in the trio of the masks in the Act I finale.

None the less, Don Giovanni's descent into hell is properly followed by an epilogue, omitted in the later nineteenth and early twentieth centuries in deference to the romantic view that damnation on moral grounds must be greeted with a straight face. To be fair to those who cut it, it was omitted by Mozart himself for the Viennese performances of 1788, but this was most probably because there was not only an additional aria for Elvira, but also an added scene for Zerlina and Leporello (invariably cut nowadays), which made the opera too long. All stylistic logic pleads for the inclusion of the epilogue, which starts seriously enough, but points the moral in a way consistent with the idea of the *dramma giocoso* Mozart and da Ponte thought they had written.

Don Giovanni's fascination lies partly in its almost unlimited ambition; partly in its ambivalent balance between high comedy and even higher seriousness; partly in what we may perceive as the element of imperfection which results from ambition and

The Cemetery Scene at Glyndebourne in 1951, with Mario Petri (Don Giovanni), Alois Pernerstorfer (Leporello) and Bruce Dargavel (the Commendatore).

John Piper's design (1951) for the Cemetery Scene, which reveals that there had been some second thoughts before it was realised for the stage.

ambiguity alike. With almost none of its principal figures may we, with any continuing hold on real life, attempt to identify – not the scolding Donna Elvira, the glacial Donna Anna, the priggish Don Ottavio, the flirtatious and spiteful Zerlina, the cloddish Masetto, the time-serving Leporello, perhaps not even the protagonist, however dashing his behaviour and keen his sense of humour. Some extra quality would have to be suggested for each of them,

except maybe for Don Giovanni, who may plead in mitigation his search for the perfect woman with whom he may finally find contentment. Yet the opera's aspirations are so high, its musical level so hard to parallel, that any audience will applaud the attempt eventually to iron out the flaws and square the circle, so that *Don Giovanni* may stand revealed as what so many have in the past enjoyed claiming it to be – the perfect opera.

WOLFGANG AMADEUS MOZART

Così fan tutte

So Do All Women

Opera buffa in two acts by Mozart, text by Lorenzo da Ponte. First performed at the Burgtheater, Vienna on January 26, 1790, with Ferrarese del Bene, Villeneuve (who were sisters in real life), Dorotea Bussani, Calvesi, Benucci and Signor Bussani.

CHARACTERS

Fiordiligi, *a Neapolitan lady*	Soprano
Dorabella, *her sister*	Soprano
Ferrando, *Dorabella's fiancé*	Tenor
Guglielmo, *engaged to Fiordiligi*	Bass
Don Alfonso, *a bachelor*	Baritone
Despina, *maid to Fiordiligi and Dorabella*	Soprano

Time: Eighteenth century
Place: Naples
Approx Act Lengths: Act I 84 min., Act II 83 min.

Così fan tutte, ossia La Scuola degli Amanti was written by Mozart to a commission from the Emperor Joseph II; the story is said to have been based on a real-life incident. Two young officers are so sure of the constancy of the sisters to whom they are engaged that they make a bet with an older bachelor friend, who insists that a woman's memory is shorter than they would ever believe. They swear not to give the game away, then disguise themselves as Albanians and, having obtained the assistance of Despina, the maid, start to make advances to each other's fiancée. After an apparently valiant show of resistance which lasts the whole of the finale of Act I and well into Act II, the sisters succumb and swap partners. But at the wedding party all is revealed and the young men reappear in their original uniforms.

The story's symmetrical set-up – two pairs of lovers, a third of worldly-wise cynics – provides Mozart with opportunities not only for incomparable music, but also for comment on the surface comedy and the heartbreak which lies beneath a role-swapping joke that goes too far and

constantly risks – even welcomes – taking a serious turn. Nineteenth-century taste, beginning with Beethoven, found the theme either immoral or inconsequential and went out of its way to provide the music with a new libretto, a futile exercise in view of the quality and sophistication of da Ponte's original.

By the time he wrote *Così*, Mozart had gone as far as seems possible along a line which had become peculiarly his own and which no-one else was to explore either so deeply or so fruitfully, based on his conviction that nothing in real life is ever quite so simple as it appears, not so happy, not so tragic. The musical expression of this ambivalence was a challenge he could never resist, whether imposed on him by his librettist or sought after because he relished the situation so much. Already in *Figaro* and even more so in *Don Giovanni*, he had mined this vein – think of Figaro's aria early in the last act when he does not quite know whether to be wholly outraged that Susanna may be unfaithful or uncomfortably amused that he, the arch-intriguer,

Above: *Hilde Güden (Despina) with Petre Munteanu (Ferrando) and Erich Kunz (Guglielmo) at Glyndebourne in 1948.*

Right: *Sena Jurinac as Fiordiligi in Vienna.*

could have watched and laughed at his wife making an assignation under his very nose. Or remember Leporello in *Don Giovanni*, gibbering with fear and inviting to supper the Commendatore's statue, which answers with great solemnity, while Don Giovanni, however impressed at the turn of events, can't resist sending the whole thing up sky-high.

In *Così* this tendency is epitomised in the great scene between Fiordiligi and Ferrando not long before the start of the finale of Act II. Fiordiligi sees a last chance of extricating herself from what she perceives is an impossible situation and she sends for a uniform before announcing her intention of following her fiancé to the wars. She launches into what is obviously the opening of a grandiose aria, but this is hardly under way when the disguised Ferrando insists that before she leave she run her

sword through his heart. The proclamation of independence finishes as a love duet which has, moreover, a meltingly lovely tune suggesting not only that Fiordiligi's resistance is finished, but that something has gone seriously wrong with the whole charade. Mozart is not overreaching himself; perhaps Ferrando *is* finding himself more in love with love than with either his fiancée Dorabella or her sister; the joke has *certainly* turned entirely serious. The richness and beauty of the music only point up the unease beneath the surface which insists that you cannot joke about feelings and that the masquerade has turned real – a twist music can effect within a few bars and one which Mozart delighted in making.

At the start of the opera he has set the scene in ensemble music of incomparable delicacy and

Above: *Watched by Alfonso, the lovers make their melodious farewells in John Copley's Covent Garden production.*

Above right: *The disguised Ferrando threatens suicide: Ryland Davies, with Kiri Te Kanawa as Fiordiligi.*

Below right: *Alfonso introduces the disguised lovers to Despina in Opera Factory's updated setting, 1988.*

sensuousness, as the two young men defend the honour of their lady-loves, while Alfonso suggests things are not quite as they think. The young men are obviously convinced that their love is no mere infatuation, Don Alfonso puts his sceptical point of view with dry humour and by the end of the scene the orchestra has twice cut loose with a tune of an infectious gaiety even Mozart never surpassed.

When they are introduced in their turn, the sisters have clarinets murmuring exquisitely in thirds over strings as they day-dream about their young men. In a pair of quintets separated by two shorter numbers the new situation (which has the men going off to the wars) is broached; the ladies turn out to be inconsolable; and protracted, wonderfully melli-fluous farewells are eventually taken. All this Mozart can take in his stride, but what follows others might not have attempted. First, Don Alfonso joins Fiordiligi and Dorabella in a trio of startling beauty ('Soave sia il vento', May the breeze be gentle): since their grief appears real, even their tormentor dares not disturb the idyllic mood. But not for a bar does it survive their departure, as Don Alfonso launches into an orchestrally accompanied tirade against the whole female sex, providing the one inescapably bitter moment of the score.

Perhaps it is not inappropriate to remind oneself that Mozart fell in love with the singer Aloysia Weber, was rejected and married her sister, Constanze, so that the opera's artificial situation had for him some parallel in real life. One would hardly suggest that *Così* is the operatic equivalent of a *roman à clef*, but there is a punning reference in the second finale to the singing sisters as the 'dame Ferraresi'. In addition, Fiordiligi's magnificent aria, 'Come scoglio' ('Firm as rock'), has a slight air of parody and its prodigious range, extensive coloratura and leaps up and down the full compass of the soprano voice were, it has been thought, intended not only to display the original performer's technique, but also to poke fun at her: she was da Ponte's mistress and a formidable singer, but apparently not in Mozart's best books.

The comedy of *Così fan tutte*, like all comedy of genius, comments profoundly and movingly on the human condition and it does so in the most consistently mellifluous operatic music Mozart ever wrote.

WOLFGANG AMADEUS MOZART

Die Zauberflöte

The Magic Flute

Opera in two acts by Mozart, text by Emmanuel Schikaneder (and, probably, Ludwig Giesecke). The text of this *Zauberoper*[1] was outlined by March 1791. Mozart worked on the music until July, at which point he broke off to concentrate on his Requiem and *La clemenza di Tito*. By the end of September he had completed the music and on September 30, 1791 the première took place in Vienna at the Theater auf der Wieden. Nanetta Gottlieb (Pamina), Josepha Hofer[2] (Queen of the Night), Schack (Tamino), Gerl (Sarastro) and of course Schikaneder himself (Papageno) led the cast. The opera had considerable success, but Mozart died on December 5 of the same year.

CHARACTERS

Tamino, *a Prince*	Tenor
Three Ladies, *in attendance on the Queen of the Night*	Two sopranos, Mezzo-soprano
Papageno, *a bird-catcher*	Baritone
The Queen of the Night	Soprano
Monostatos, *a Moor in Sarastro's service*	Tenor
Pamina, *daughter of the Queen of the Night*	Soprano
Three Genii	Two sopranos, Mezzo-soprano
The Speaker, *in the service of the Temple*	Bass
Sarastro, *High Priest of Isis and Osiris*	Bass
Two Priests	Tenor, Bass
Papagena	Soprano
Two men in armour	Tenor, Bass

Slaves, Priests, People, etc.

Time: Legendary
Place: Egypt
Approx Act Lengths: Act I 66 min., Act II 82 min.

Like many of the great figures of the eighteenth century – Voltaire, Goethe, Haydn and possibly Beethoven – Mozart and Schikaneder were freemasons: masonic ritual features in both the text and the music of *Die Zauberflöte*. So do references to historical figures who favoured or opposed masonry, including the implacably hostile Roman Catholic Church: the Queen of the Night has been identified with the old Empress Maria Theresa, Tamino with the young Emperor Joseph II, Monostatos with the Jesuits, and so on. Freemasonry was seen by its enemies as a vehicle of liberal thought as it obtained in England and France: in France, moreover, it was

1. An opera concerned with magic and exploiting magic's stage possibilities.

2. *Née* Weber, she was the eldest sister of Mozart's wife, Constanze

thought to have been a contributory cause of the Revolution. There is little doubt that to show masonry in a good light, particularly at a time when it was under considerable threat, was one of the objectives of *Die Zauberflöte*'s creators. This was the reason, it has been argued, why masons had no objection to elements of their ritual, usually a strict secret, being seen in public.

Schikaneder was not only a freemason, but a highly successful comedian and theatrical impresario and the opera's swing between comedy and high seriousness derives partly from the popular nature of his German-language theatre, partly from his personal style (in the twentieth century he would have been a television personality) and partly from the catchy tunes Mozart knew how to write for him. Apparently at the opposite pole to all this is the pull Mozart felt towards the serious side of life, identified at least partly with the freemasonry whose liberalising influence he and Schikaneder were so keen to defend.

The overture starts with the famous three masonic chords and a dozen bars of grave *adagio* music: with them is contrasted a brisk *allegro* theme which hints at the lighter side of the opera associated later with Papageno.

Act I.   Tamino rushes in pursued by a serpent. He sinks down exhausted, but three ladies enter and kill his attacker with their spears. In an extended trio they show that each of them is fascinated by the handsome prince and would like the other two to go for help while she remains by his side. In the end they all depart and Tamino revives alone and is amazed at the sight of the dead snake. He is intrigued by the sound of pipes in the distance and then by the sight of a man dancing in covered in feathers. Schikaneder played Papageno and Mozart gave him lively music to sing, of which his entrance song, 'Der Vogelfänger bin ich ja' (I am the jolly bird-catcher) with its piping refrain is an excellent example. Papageno claims to have killed the serpent and saved Tamino, but the Ladies laugh at his lie, punishing him by padlocking his lips. They then give Tamino a portrait of the daughter of the Queen of the Night, their mistress.

Tamino immediately falls in love (aria: 'Dies

The Ladies kill the dragon: Glyndebourne, 1978. David Hockney designed the production.

The Queen of Night's appearance, designed by Karl Friedrich Schinkel, Berlin, 1815.

Bildnis ist bezaubernd schön', This picture is amazing fair). Pamina is a prisoner of the wicked Sarastro, say the Ladies, and no sooner has Tamino, the epitome of noble ardour, sworn to rescue her than the Queen herself materialises, singing of her desolation at the loss of her daughter and urging him to rescue her. The writing for the Queen here and in her second aria is full of coloratura and ascents into the soprano stratosphere (one top F now, four at her next appearance), but the music is urgent and grandly dramatic and represents a great challenge to a high soprano.

In a quintet the Ladies release Papageno from his padlock, giving him a set of chiming bells and Tamino a flute. With this supernatural aid, they will survive all dangers and three Genii will guide them on their journey to free Pamina. The music associated with these supernatural beings has a peculiarly powerful 'stillness' to which only the word 'magical' can appropriately be applied. If *Die Zauberflöte* has transcendental qualities – and who can doubt it? - this music and what flows from it constitute the magic's most sublime expression.

We move to 'a magnificent Egyptian room' into which Monostatos drags a protesting Pamina. She faints, but the appearance of Papageno puts the Moor to flight. Papageno recognises Pamina and assures her that she will soon be rescued by a man who has already fallen in love with her portrait – not the kind of thing which ever happens to *him*, he laments. Pamina comforts him and they sing gently and innocently of love (duet: 'Bei Männern, welche Liebe fühlen', Amongst men, whoever feels the force of love).

The finale is set in front of three Temples, inscribed to Wisdom, Reason and Nature. To ethereal music the Genii lead in Tamino, who apostrophises the temples as if he means to learn their secrets. The central door opens to reveal the Speaker, who engages the young man in weighty discussion and informs him that Sarastro is no tyrant, but a wise man of noble character. Tamino

Helen Field (Pamina) and John Rawnsley (Papageno) in Nicholas Hytner's production for English National Opera.

soliloquises, his seemingly rhetorical questions being answered by an unseen chorus. He takes his flute and plays (aria: 'Wie stark ist nicht dein Zauberton', How strongly sounds your magic tone), drawing wild animals to him by the charm of his playing. Before the end of his aria he hears Papageno's pipes in the distance and runs off to find him.

Papageno leads in Pamina. Their duet is punctuated by Papageno's pipes and the sound of Tamino's answering flute, until Monostatos catches up with them, accompanied by a group of slaves, and seems to have taken them prisoner. In the nick of time Papageno remembers his magic bells, the sound of which sends the slaves dancing off into the distance. Pamina and Papageno rejoice at their escape, but trumpets announce the arrival of Sarastro. Pamina takes charge – they will tell Sarastro nothing but the truth, she says – and throws herself at his feet, begging for forgiveness that, under provocation, she attempted to escape. Sarastro comforts her: he understands her predicament and the gods will provide a remedy. Monostatos drags in Tamino. While he and Pamina

are greeting each other rapturously, Monostatos is exposed to Sarastro as a fraud and a bully and sent off for punishment. On Sarastro's orders the two young lovers are led to the Temple to prove that they are worthy of the higher happiness.

Act II. The Priests of the Temple enter to a march, whose dark, serious tone colours much of the ensuing act. The masonic chords are heard again and Sarastro announces that the gods have decided that Pamina shall become the wife of Tamino: he must undergo purification and she will remain under his protection. Sarastro prays in music of the utmost solemnity and beauty that wisdom may be theirs (aria: 'O Isis und Osiris', O Isis and Osiris).

Tamino's ordeals begin with that of Silence. Rolling thunder interrupts Papageno's attempt to put a bold face on things and two Priests warn them to be on their guard against women's wiles: indeed, were it not for the valiant-for-truth figure of Pamina, *Die Zauberflöte* might well become a target for the wrath of liberated women. When the Priests disappear, the seekers are then confronted with the three Ladies, who try to dissuade them from their quest.

Sarastro (Gwynne Howell) leads his priests in Act II of English National Opera's production in 1988, designed by Bob Crowley.

Monostatos reappears to lust over the sleeping Pamina, but is put to flight by the entry of the Queen. She flings her daughter a dagger with orders to kill Sarastro and launches into the most famous of coloratura arias, whose rapid, dagger-sharp *staccato* writing suggests boiling hatred far more than a mere vehicle for vocal display ('Der Hölle Rache kocht in meinem Herzen', A hellish fury rages in my heart). Monostatos believes he has caught Pamina red-handed, but Sarastro sends him packing and assures Pamina that revenge on her mother is far from his mind (aria: 'In diesen heil'gen Hallen', Within these sacred walls). Again, the nobility of the musical expression suggests a man of rare and forgiving humanity.

The trials are resumed. Papageno chatters away to an old crone who tells him, much to his discomfiture, that she is his sweetheart, Papagena. A clap of thunder, and she is replaced by the three Genii, bringing food and drink together with the flute and bells and singing in the same vein as when we first encountered them – a 'hit' number, apparently, from the time of the first performance.

Pamina joins the two aspirants, overjoyed to have found Tamino again. When she is greeted with silence she seems to lose her belief in human constancy. Her aria ('Ach, ich fühl's', Ah, it is gone) is in Mozart's tragic key of G minor and its mixture of maturity and innocence together with extremes of grief is consistent with that picture of ideal feminity which Mozart and Schikaneder have been building up.

The scene changes to the interior of the Temple, where the Priests sing in explicitly masonic terms of the retreat of darkness before the brilliance of light. Soon Tamino is led in to be congratulated on his steadfastness. Pamina follows him and in a beautiful trio ('Soll ich dich, Teurer, nicht mehr seh'n?', Shall I not see you again, my dearest?) they are told to take their last farewells.

Now it is Papageno's turn, but his choice of wine for a last wish seems to leave him vaguely unsatisfied. In a merry song ('Ein Mädchen oder Weibchen', A girl or a little wife) he makes it clear what is missing, an increasingly exuberant glockenspiel adding spice between the verses. The old woman reappears and threatens Papageno with dire punishment if he does not swear eternal fidelity.

Papageno's last appeal (Thomas Allen at Covent Garden).

When he does she then reveals herself as the comeliest of prospective mates – but a Priest whisks her away from the expostulating Papageno.

The opera's long and varied finale is introduced by the Genii, who sing of the symbolical joys of the rising sun; the hushed beauty of their music conveys a sense of being 'different' and a feeling of dedication, one of the major characteristics of the serious side of *Die Zauberflöte*. Pamina is in the last stages of despair and, not knowing she is observed, she attempts suicide. The Genii comfort her in music of extraordinary tenderness.

Two Men in Armour preside over the last stages of the initiation. Tamino is brought in to face the trials of Fire and Water, which are heralded by a chorale prelude sung by the Men in Armour together while the orchestra elaborates a *fugato*. Tamino's resolution is redoubled when Pamina's voice is heard outside. She becomes his guide through the final ordeals and their mutual tenderness and the confidence they derive from each other as they exchange musical lines bring radiance to one of the opera's greatest scenes. At the end the Priests welcome them into the Temple.

At this point occurs Papageno's aria of mock suicide. His song, 'Papagena! Papagena!', shows him in more serious mood than his earlier numbers and an appeal to the audience for one friendly voice to speak up on his behalf brings the Genii to save him. The scene ends with an irresistible patter duet for him and Papagena.

The powers of darkness in the persons of the Queen, her Ladies and Monostatos, make a last bid for control and the music momentarily takes on a sinister colouring. But soon Sarastro appears to dispel the darkness and to welcome Pamina and Tamino into the realm of the Sun.

The genius of Mozart and the theatrical know-how of Schikaneder have combined to make an opera which is unique. In the end, it is not the succession of arias, magnificent as they are, which gives the work its flavour; rather it is the way it reconciles Papageno's comedy of the common man with the universal theme of darkness dispelled by light. It is not too much to say that the combination has produced the first operatic masterpiece in demotic mode, written not for the court or the aristocracy, but for the people.

LUDWIG VAN BEETHOVEN

Fidelio

Opera in two (originally three) acts by Beethoven; text by Joseph
Sonnleithner and Georg Friedrich Sonnleithner, after Jean Nicolas
Bouilly. Première in Vienna on November 20, 1805 with Anna Milder
as Leonore and Demmer as Florestan. Revived in revised version in
March 1806 and in its final form in 1814.

CHARACTERS

Florestan, *a Spanish nobleman*	Tenor
Leonore, *his wife*	Soprano
Don Fernando, *the King's Minister*	Baritone
Don Pizarro, *Governor of the prison*	Baritone
Rocco, *chief gaoler*	Bass
Marcellina, *Rocco's daughter*	Soprano
Jacquino, *assistant to Rocco*	Tenor
Two prisoners	Tenor, Bass

Soldiers, Prisoners and People

Time: Eighteenth century
Place: Near Seville
Approx Act Lengths: Act I 74 min., Act II 48 min.

Fidelio can seem so romantic and idealised a subject
that it may be hard for a late twentieth-century
audience to believe that, for Beethoven, the subject
was essentially contemporary and was based by the
French writer of the original version of the story,
Jean Nicolas Bouilly, on experience of the French
Revolution. As if to underline this, the audience at
the première in Vienna in 1805 was mostly made up
of soldiers from the French army of occupation,
though not even Beethoven's friends seriously
argued that this was a factor in the opera's relative
lack of success.

The story is simple and straightforward. By a
trick, Don Pizarro has imprisoned his enemy, Don
Florestan, and given out that Florestan is dead.
Forestan's wife, however, has disguised herself as a
boy, assumed the name of Fidelio, and inveigled her
way into the prison service.

Act I. In the prison yard Jacquino and
Marcellina are sparring. He is in love with her, but
she prefers Fidelio, Rocco's newly hired and already
invaluable assistant (aria: 'O wär' ich schon mit dir
vereint', O were I already married to you). Fidelio
offers to accompany Rocco to the dungeon where a
'special' prisoner is kept and Rocco accepts. A
march announces the arrival of Don Pizarro who has
word that the Minister is on his way to inspect the
prison (aria: 'Ha! welch' ein Augenblick', Ha! What
a moment) and who has resolved with Rocco's
help to do away with his enemy. Leonore, now
convinced that this prisoner is her husband (aria:
'Abscheulicher!', You monstrous fiend!), persuades
Rocco to allow the other prisoners out into the sun,
but on Pizarro's reappearance they are hustled back
into their cells.

Act II. Florestan is alone in his dungeon (aria:
'Gott! welch' Dunkel hier', God! How dark it is in
here), but is joined by Rocco and Fidelio who have
come to dig his grave (trio: 'Euch werde Lohn', May
you have reward). Don Pizarro makes a move to kill

Julius Patzak, the greatest of post-war Florestans, Salzburg, 1949.

Lotte Lehmann, a great pre-war Leonore, Salzburg, 1936.

him (quartet: 'Er sterbe! Doch er soll erst wissen', He'll die! But he first must know), but this is thwarted when Fidelio throws himself between the two men and reveals herself as Leonore. The Minister's arrival is heralded by Jacquino and in the last scene Don Fernando arrests Pizarro and, amid general rejoicing, watches Leonore remove Florestan's fetters.

The original version of *Fidelio*, nowadays referred to as *Leonore*, dates from 1805 and had text by the Sonnleithners. Breuning had a hand in the 1806 revision, which reduced three acts to two, and

the more experienced Treitschke contributed dramaturgical advice and substantially revised the text for the final version of 1814. There was also musical revision of every number except Pizarro's march in Act I. A comparison between the composer's first and last thoughts is revealing, and a performance of *Leonore* (revived by Sadler's Wells Opera, for instance, for the Beethoven bi-centenary in 1970) or even a recording will show that Beethoven's initial attempts were far from negligible. It will also demonstrate the improvement that came with a maturer view – I cannot accept

Ernest Newman's notion that the resigned, *andante* second section of Florestan's aria in the original was preferable to the hallucinated and feverish ending Beethoven supplied in 1814. One is dramatically apt, the other a stroke of nothing less than genius.

The truth is that, in spite of his interest in the form and his keenness to continue to write for the stage, Beethoven in his first (and only) opera had set himself a hard problem. His natural inclination was towards high-minded, heroic themes, but the form in which he was writing was the less elevated *Singspiel*, the German term for opera with spoken dialogue: a reconciliation between these two ideas was a tall order. In any version, the first scene of Act II, in Florestan's dungeon, demonstrates Beethoven's innate instinct for drama, but the first act is guided for the most part by the *Singspiel* convention; and it is a skilful conductor (and producer) who succeeds in marrying the stylistic demands of Beethoven's music, some of which is on the grandest scale – the quartet, for example, and Leonore's 'Abscheulicher!' – and Bouilly's and Sonnleithner's drama, much of which, with its sometimes banal dialogue, verges on the domestic in layout and expression.

From the opera's outset, the composer's best instincts come into play and the no-nonsense overture (written for the third version of the opera) is full of anticipatory movement – what E. M. Forster once described as the 'and then?' factor in story-telling. The opening scene makes good use of the *Singspiel* convention, with the *terzetto* for Fidelio, Marcellina and Rocco, and Pizarro's aria pushing it to the limit without losing its advantages. Too serious

Neil Howlett (Pizarro), Josephine Barstow (Leonore) and Alberto Remedios (Florestan): E.N.O., 1980.

to fit the category are the great canon quartet, Leonore's aria and much of the finale. Beethoven anticipates the lofty aspirations of Act II most of all, perhaps, with his prisoners as they grope their way towards the light with that mixture of hope and resignation which somehow attaches to all who are prisoners of war or of conscience and have not been through the criminal courts. (A common production gloss in the late twentieth century has been to suggest – with some dramatic, but less musical justification – that by no means all the inmates of Don Pizarro's gaol are as innocent as Florestan.)

In Act II, Beethoven finds himself on home territory. No more dramatic an opening could be imagined than the extraordinary introduction to the dungeon scene, with its heavily weighted chords, grinding turns on the strings and apparently endless descent into the depths until the tenor's G shines from the darkness out of the chord. It is followed by a wonderful piece of word-setting in the arioso-recitative, a passage of nervous, rudderless despair; the aria itself, however racked, returns to the relative security of recollection of time past, until in the quick section any grasp of normality is relinquished and what starts as Florestan's vision of Leonore ends in pure hysteria. Music cannot get any bleaker than the opening of this scene, but it would not be Beethoven if it did not contain a ray of hope, a prospect of superhuman endeavour leading to ultimate triumph.

In this great scene we return to the world of 'and then?' with the duet for Leonore and Rocco, only to revert immediately to the higher drama with an agonised string attack at the start of the trio, which precisely echoes Leonore's equally agonised spoken exclamation: 'His voice tugs at the very strings of your heart'. The snatches of spoken dialogue between the music achieve dramatic continuity more surely than in Act I: the test comes with the ferocious drama of the quartet and the release of tension provided by the duet, 'O namenlose Freude' (O nameless joy), as exuberant in its context as the plunging of an unleashed horse.

Leonore is, of course, the opera's central character, a heroic figure with her strong affirmation of 'Ich habe Muth' (I have courage) in the first act trio; her great aria of protest against injustice; to say

nothing of those memorable cries of 'Noch heute' in the first act finale at the prospect of seeing Florestan that day and of 'Tödt erst sein Weib!' (First kill his wife!) in the denouement of Act II as she interposes herself between the would-be murderer and his intended victim. Through the years, and depending on your point of view, she has come to stand for all

Don Fernando (Robert Lloyd) sends for Pizarro (Donald McIntyre): Covent Garden, 1983.

gallant women and all strivers for freedom.

Performances of *Fidelio* contain a problem, that of the inclusion or omission of the overture known as *Leonore No. 3*, the finest of the three overtures Beethoven wrote for the various versions of *Leonore*. It has been used to cover the scene change in Act II, a practice regularised (but apparently not invented) by Mahler in Vienna. I believe it is to be deplored, partly because in different form the overture repeats much of the scene it follows and partly because the effect of resolution which the finale's key of C major

The finale of Act II in Joachim Herz's production for English National Opera, 1985.

can produce disappears if that key has been hammering away for some minutes beforehand. But the principal objection to the practice is that it destroys the dramatic balance of the entire act. The musicologist Edward Dent once rather wickedly suggested that the piece be played at the opera's end for those for whom *Fidelio* would not be complete without it and for prima donna conductors who must play it!

In recent years, either *Fidelio* or *Die Meistersinger* (and, just occasionally, *Die Zauberflöte*) has become an obligatory element of German festive occasions, whether the opening of a new opera house or the greeting of an official visitor. It is hard to think of a better work for such an occasion than Beethoven's solitary opera, with its exalted theme and its testimony to the composer's way with drama. It is the only one of the operas treated in this volume which is not by an experienced or highly professional opera composer, but you are reminded each time you hear it that it is something like a tragedy that Beethoven never wrote another.

GIOACCHINO ANTONIO ROSSINI

Il barbiere di Siviglia

The Barber of Seville

Opera in two acts by Rossini; text by Sterbini founded on Beaumarchais's play *Le Barbier de Séville*. Rossini's contract for *Il Barbiere* (called initially *Almaviva ossia l'Inutile Precauzione* in deference to Paisiello's *Barbiere* of 1782) was signed in Rome on December 15, 1815, nine weeks before the première, and according to Rossini, he spent thirteen days writing the score (nineteen according to the estimate of Giuseppe Radiciotti, Rossini's biographer). Its first performance, on February 20, 1816 at the Teatro Argentina in Rome, had Giorgi-Righetti as Rosina, Manuel Garcia[1] as Count Almaviva and Luigi Zamboni as Figaro, but the evening was a fiasco, with an apparently hostile public and a full bag of stage mishaps.

CHARACTERS

Count Almaviva, *a nobleman*	Tenor
Doctor Bartolo	Basso buffo
Don Basilio, *a singing teacher*	Bass
Figaro, *a barber*	Baritone
Fiorello, *servant to the Count*	Bass
Ambrogio, *servant to the doctor*	Bass
Rosina, *the doctor's ward*	Mezzo-soprano
Berta, *Rosina's governess*	Soprano

Notary, Constable, Musicians and Soldiers

Time: Seventeenth century
Place: Seville
Approx Act Lengths: Act I 97 min., Act II 53 min.

The overture, with its skilful mixture of lyrical and chattering themes backed up by energetic crescendos, is one of Rossini's most famous and had earlier done duty for his *Aureliano in Palmira* (1813) and *Elisabetta, Regina d'Inghilterra* (1815) – neither apparently successful enough to prevent Rossini using it again – so that it has no connection either with Seville or with themes appearing later in the opera.

Act I.   At dawn, outside Doctor Bartolo's house, Count Almaviva serenades his unknown beloved (aria: 'Ecco ridente in cielo', See, smiling in the sky).

He hears from Figaro, who arrives opportunely (aria: 'Largo al factotum della città', Make way for the busiest man in town), that Rosina is Doctor Bartolo's ward and that Bartolo plans to marry her himself. Almaviva sings again, announcing himself, falsely but perhaps prudently, as Lindoro (aria: 'Se il mio nome', If my name you would know). The Count and Figaro plot the next move (duet in two sections: 'All' idea di quel metallo', For an idea of

1. Father of two famous prima donnas, Maria Malibran and Pauline Viardot.

Adelina Patti, a famous soprano Rosina.

Giuseppe de Luca, a celebrated Figaro throughout his career.

quite such brilliance/'Numero quindici', At number fifteen).

Inside Doctor Bartolo's house Rosina suggests that she is sweetness and light until crossed, when she becomes the very devil (aria: 'Una voce poco fà', A little voice within my heart). From now on, nothing is straightforward, all is intrigue. Bartolo hears Basilio suggest that Rosina's admirer could be got rid of by spreading slander (aria: 'La calunnia è un venticello', Slander is like a breath of wind); Rosina sends her lover a letter by Figaro; and her guardian rounds off the scene by giving her a thorough scolding for deceit (aria: 'A un dottor della mia sorte', To a doctor of my importance). In the finale Bartolo is confronted with a drunken soldier demanding a billet (Almaviva in disguise). Berta and Basilio join the ensemble before the arrival of the watch, who attempt to arrest the Count, but desist when they see the paper he produces. Doctor Bartolo is dumbfounded (ensemble: 'Fredda ed immobile', Frozen and motionless).

Act II. Doctor Bartolo wonders whether the drunken soldier could be Count Almaviva, but his house is invaded by a music-master, whose reiterated greeting ('Pace e gioia sia con voi', Peace and joy be now upon you) soon has the doctor hopping with irritation. The newcomer says he is Don Alonso, come to give Rosina a music lesson in

Doctor Bartolo (Claudio Desderi) and the disguised Almaviva (Max-René Cosotti): Glyndebourne, 1981.

place of his sick master, Don Basilio. Rosina contrives not to betray that she knows who Don Alonso is and sings to his accompaniment (the 'Music Lesson' Scene). Figaro and the disguised Count save the day when Don Basilio arrives and the Count's offer of money persuades him to go home (ensemble: 'Buona sera, mio signore', Good night, my good sir). Bartolo smells a plot and packs the others off, vowing he will marry Rosina then and there and put an end to the intrigues. He persuades Rosina that Lindoro is a decoy to lure her into Count Almaviva's clutches, so that, after a storm interlude, she is in no mood to welcome the Count and Figaro when they appear for the planned elopement. They effect a reconciliation (trio: 'Ah! qual colpo', Ah, what a stroke). Their escape ladder disappears, but Don Basilio is easily pressured into witnessing the betrothal of Rosina and the Count; and poor Bartolo has to put as good a face on things as he can contrive.

In spite of the disaster of its first night, *Barbiere* was much admired by both Beethoven and Verdi; and to later opera-goers it has seemed the quintessence of Italian comedy, good-natured and sunny, full of complications and yet direct, with a profusion of melody whose grace and elegance are matched only by its wit, energy and comic *élan*. Over the decades the opera has stood the test of acting as everything from a display framework for star singers to an operatic introduction for beginners and Rossini's pedigree for comedy seems to have been by the *Commedia dell'arte* out of the last movements of Haydn's symphonies and quartets, with Beethoven acting perhaps as none too approving godfather.

For much of the nineteenth century, the opera was treated as a vehicle for singers, with many of the arias, famous as they are, encrusted with decoration as generations of singers tried to outdo each other.

When aspirants came to sing to him, Rossini used sometimes to pretend not to recognise what they had sung; and for more than a hundred years after the opera's première, the 'Music Lesson' Scene was quite falsely given out to have been lost so that singers could substitute favourite songs and arias to show off their prowess. Even the original Rosina substituted her own selections for Rossini's Lesson aria and later prima donnas sang music of any period, including some written after the opera's

The disguised Almaviva persuades Basilio he really is ill: Bartolo (Ian Wallace), Almaviva (Juan Oncina), Basilio (Antonio Cassinelli), Rosina (Graziella Sciutti) and Figaro (Sesto Bruscantini), Glyndebourne, 1954.

time: Patti liked to conclude with 'Home, sweet home' and Melba and Sembrich with a song to which each played her own accompaniment. The last three were sopranos and for most of the last century, and much of this, sopranos sang Rosina with conspicuous success. But the role was written for a flexible middle voice, based rather low, and using the higher register for decoration and as the exception rather than the rule. Unless upwardly transposed, as it used to be for something like a hundred years, it sits best for mezzo-soprano or low-based soprano (Maria Callas and Victoria de los Angeles sang it as easily as Giulietta Simionato or Teresa Berganza).

There are four other splendid roles besides Rosina's. Don Basilio, a much shorter role than that of Bartolo, belongs to a straight bass, but his 'slander' aria is a wonderful invention: Slander, he says, starts as a gentle breeze (the orchestra echoes the idea), then swells to a mighty roar like a cannon. The orchestra has a slow crescendo and the voice describes the effect of the firing of the gun. The role of Bartolo is much longer and though often sung by a *buffo* bass is better suited to a strong character baritone. His aria in the second scene of Act I, when he accuses Rosina of dropping a note from her window, is *buffo* writing on a vast scale.

The Count's music is an object lesson in writing for the *tenore di grazia* – polished and nimble, but also replete with wit and character. His two solos at the start of Act I are full of grace and coloratura flourishing, the second being one of Rossini's most delightful inventions. To sing this kind of music was once within the power of any leading lyric tenor, but it is now the province of specialists, few of whom seem able to sing it with the ease and musical effectiveness brought to it before and after 1900 by, for instance, the great Fernando de Lucia, whose recordings exist to prove the point. Figaro's is a more obviously brilliant role, on the whole high but not especially light in tone. His entrance aria, 'Largo al factotum', is one of the most memorable tongue-twisters in operatic literature. Figaro is not only the town's barber and chief busybody (a portrait of the writer Beaumarchais himself), but also a man of extraordinary energy who makes sure that his light is never hidden beneath a bushel.

The opera's perennial appeal is, however, not mainly due to its arias or to what it can offer to singers – though it needs and sometimes still gets fine singing. As a whole it is wonderfully consistent, perhaps because of the speed with which Rossini wrote it and for which he was subsequently mocked. Characters are set up in the twinkling of an eye and developed with just as much precision – in fact, so strong is the framework Rossini establishes that there is something almost foolproof about *Barbiere*. The opportunities he gives singers seem only to push their impulses in the right direction.

Real operatic comedy is rarer than one imagines and even in Mozart more often means a matching of music to a comic situation than actual musical wit (Beethoven explodes, Mozart insinuates, others have bassoon jokes, but only Rossini continually bubbles and chuckles). Each of Almaviva's disguised entrances provides an example of Rossini's comic invention. The mock drunk aiming to get billeted in a house which has exemption, or the nervous music-teacher with his over-serious 'Pace e gioia', a tune which gets going so well that he seems to forget how to change gear – both are quite different in musical character from the high spirits of the Almaviva-Figaro duet in Act I or the Count's well-timed asides to Rosina when he is himself and not in disguise.

This comic gift is at its best in Act I's great finale. The watch arrives in Bartolo's house and everyone tries to explain his or her view of the situation: a scatty ensemble builds up, to the obvious bewilderment of the officer who attempts to arrest the Count. The production of a piece of paper commands instant deference and leaves Bartolo so totally nonplussed that an ensemble of deft wit develops as he stands, all motion suspended, while the others comment on a situation which is a classic of absurdity. Once the succeeding *stretta* gets going, there seems no reason why Rossini's repetitions should ever end and the music gets faster and faster until, with many a crescendo, it comes to a rousing finish.

In the end, the theme of the guardian outwitted and young love triumphant is basic to comedy and *Barbiere* pushes it for all it is worth. But the opera would not be so famous if the music were not so witty and, I am tempted to say, so wise.

Telramund lies at Lohengrin's mercy after the duel. This painting must have been made only a few years after the opera's première in 1850.

RICHARD WAGNER

Lohengrin

Opera in three acts, words and music by Richard Wagner. The text was completed by the end of 1845; the music, starting with the third act, before the end of August 1847; and the orchestration at the end of March 1848. The first performance was on August 28, 1850, conducted by Liszt, with Agthe, Fasztlinger, Beck, Feodor von Milde and Höfer. Wagner himself, because of complicity in the 1849 rising in Saxony, did not hear the opera until 1861 in Vienna.

CHARACTERS

Henry the Fowler, *King of Saxony*	Bass
Lohengrin	Tenor
Elsa of Brabant	Soprano
Duke Gottfried, *her brother*	Silent
Friedrich von Telramund, *Count of Brabant*	Baritone
Ortrud, *his wife*	Mezzo-soprano
The King's Herald	Baritone

Saxon, Thuringian and Brabantian Nobles; Ladies of Honour; Pages; Attendants

Time: Early tenth century
Place: Antwerp
Approx Act Lengths: Act I 64 min., Act II 86 min., Act III 62 min.

After the considerable success of *Der fliegende Holländer*, Wagner had finished *Tannhäuser* (first performed in October 1845) and was on a convalescent holiday during the summer when, almost simultaneously and as a result of his holiday reading, the subjects of *Lohengrin* and *Die Meistersinger von Nürnberg* came to his attention. He had completed a scenario for the latter before becoming captivated to the exclusion of everything else by the romantic subject of *Lohengrin*.

Part of the opera's basis is historical and concerned with King Henry I of Saxony, who not only defended Germany against hostile elements from the East but greatly extended his domain to create an empire in all but name. More important is the basis in myth – the legend of Lohengrin and the Swan, the knight coming to the rescue of a maiden in distress, the child transformed by magic into a swan, and the guardian of the Grail allowed to descend to the world of men for noble purposes, but not allowed to become part of it.

Act I. King Henry of Saxony is attempting to restructure the defence of Germany and in particular to secure the allegiance of Brabant against his enemies, with whom his treaty has expired. Telramund heads the Brabantian nobles and, before the King, accuses his ward, Elsa, of having murdered her brother, Gottfried. Elsa relates a dream (aria: 'Einsam in trüben Tagen', Once in my lonely days): a knight will come to champion her against her accusers. Lohengrin mysteriously appears in a boat drawn by a swan. If Elsa will take him as her champion, he must first obtain her solemn promise never to question him as to his name and origin. Elsa accepts the condition, which is twice enunciated: 'Nie sollst du mich befragen',

Ernst Kraus as Lohengrin in the early 1900s.

Never may you question me. Lohengrin defeats Telramund in single combat, sparing his life.

Act II.   While the King and his court carouse, Telramund and the evil Ortrud plot revenge. Elsa appears on the balcony (aria: 'Euch Lüften, die mein Klagen', You breezes who have heard me) and Ortrud sows seeds of doubt in her mind. Telramund's banishment is proclaimed and the wedding procession of Elsa and Lohengrin begins: it is interrupted by Ortrud and Telramund, who accuse Lohengrin of sorcery. Lohengrin successfully appeals to the knights' faith in his achievement, but Elsa's resolve starts to falter as the King conducts the pair to the minster.

Act III.   After their wedding comes an extended love duet for Elsa and Lohengrin. Telramund bursts in on them and is killed by Lohengrin, who tells the King he cannot now lead the army in defence of Germany. In his narration (aria: 'In fernem Land', In a far-off land) he tells of the Grail and its knights: Parsifal is his father and he is called Lohengrin. He summons his swan (aria: 'Mein lieber Schwann', My beloved swan) and bids Elsa farewell. As Ortrud seems triumphant, Lohengrin's prayer transforms the swan into the figure of Gottfried. Elsa then sinks lifeless into her brother's arms.

Lohengrin may be seen as the culmination of Wagner's early work and the period in which, however far afield his creativity led him, he basically accepted the conventions he found to hand. Devotees can still regret that he ever abandoned this lyrical style, within which he composed with such freedom and to such effect; for with *Lohengrin* German romantic opera reaches its peak. After it, Wagner worked to different ends – with the important exception of *Meistersinger,* a sophisticated throwback to his earlier style. His break with traditional tonality, which came with *Tristan und Isolde* (first performed in 1865, but completed in 1859), is as sharp as Schoenberg's when he broke with post-Wagnerian tonality and enunciated in the years before 1914 the ideas that led to the dodecaphonic or serialist school.

Lohengrin was the last of a line and its prelude is typical of its style and aims. Whereas the overtures to *Der fliegende Holländer* and *Tannhäuser* had been concerned with the drama to come, the prelude to *Lohengrin* attempts to depict in music the Grail, its descent to earth and its subsequent return. From the Grail comes Lohengrin's commission to go to Elsa's aid; and it is because he serves it that his name must remain a secret. The mood of ecstasy the prelude suggests cannot be better encapsulated than in the opening of Wagner's own programme note: 'Out of the clear blue ether of the sky there seems to condense a wonderful yet at first hardly perceptible vision . . .' Reference to the Grail throughout the opera brings a return of this music.

The tradition within which Wagner was writing and the story he had chosen caused him to deal with calls to arms, formal proceedings, prayers,

Lohengrin (Paul Frey) defeats Telramund (Hartmut Welker) in the duel in Act I of Elijah Moshinsky's Covent Garden production.

processions and such: his music for this aspect of the opera is varied and inventive, notably the King's prayer in Act I, which develops into an impressive ensemble; the grand procession in Act II, which makes of ceremony a highly dramatic conflict; and, best of all, in Act III, the prelude, which brilliantly illustrates the wedding festivities, and the famous Wedding March, which makes an effect sure to amaze those who know it only on a church organ.

The opera's great scenes, however, are based on a different impulse which is essentially operatic in the oldest and least restrictive sense: that is to say, on a lyrical exposition of drama. The first is the scene of Lohengrin's arrival and the consequences which

flow from it. In answer to the Herald's repeated call (the Herald's role is both static and dramatically significant), Lohengrin is welcomed by the people and, in music associated with the Grail, gives thanks to the creature (aria: 'Nun sei bedankt, mein lieber Schwann', I give you thanks, my beloved swan) before announcing himself prepared to fight for Elsa's honour.

Act II starts with Telramund and Ortrud: they are drably dressed and gaze gloomily into the darkness. First Ortrud's thirst for vengeance is revealed; then Telramund's conviction that blind trust in his wife has brought him evil fortune. Ortrud's solution — tempt Elsa to ask the stranger's name and so destroy

Lohengrin (Paul Frey) and Elsa (Cheryl Studer) in the Bridal Scene at Covent Garden.

his power – wins over Telramund, superficially so strong, and fatally boosts his confidence. It is a magnificent scene of confrontation, full of drama and powerful music.

More confrontation follows. When Elsa sings softly and mellifluously to the breezes, Ortrud calls her name. She plays on Elsa's sympathies, painting a tragic picture of her and Telramund's dejection. While Elsa moves to join Ortrud, the scene changes gear abruptly: Ortrud's fury erupts and she calls on Odin and Freya, the heathen gods – whom she secretly trusts. The remainder of the scene takes place on a lower dynamic level: Ortrud wheedles her way into the confidence of Elsa, whose grasp of the

situation makes Desdemona seem acute. Few scenes for soprano and mezzo, even that for Aida and Amneris, can match this one.

Lohengrin's central episode is the love duet of Act III, where Wagner's lyrical genius reaches unequalled heights to create a chain of inspired melody during the course of which wedded bliss seems at first likely to triumph over all obstacles ('Athmest du nicht mit mir die süssen Blüme', Do you not breathe with me the scent of flowers). When Lohengrin murmurs Elsa's name, she asks to be allowed the privilege of using his in reply. Lohengrin gently puts her off and, after her repeated requests, urges her to have faith comparable to that he showed when he believed in her innocence ('Höchstes Vertrau'n', Greatest of trusts), but before Telramund's fatal entrance she is still persisting in her demands.

The last of these great lyrico-dramatic set-pieces forms the conclusion of the opera. Lohengrin reveals that Elsa's repeated questions about his identity prevent him from staying as her husband and leading the army; but he will yield to her importunity and reveal his lineage. The story of the Grail and its knights forms the burden of this narration, together with the fact that to reveal their names deprives them of their invincibility. This aria has become a justly popular solo number: many times I have heard it announced on Italian radio (not inappropriately) as the 'Romanza di *Lohengrin*'. Elsa is distraught, but when the swan can be seen returning, Lohengrin tells her that he must depart to serve the Grail.

This apotheosis of German lyricism is, paradoxically but not altogether surprisingly, often well served by Latin singers. Certainly, some of the best performances I have heard – or, at least, some of the best sung – have been in Milan or Paris. No wonder Jean de Reszke alternated the title role with those of *Faust* and *Roméo et Juliette*; nor that this was the only Wagnerian role sung by Enrico Caruso or Beniamino Gigli.

RICHARD WAGNER

Tristan und Isolde

Opera in three acts, words and music by Richard Wagner. The première took place in Munich on June 10, 1865 with Malvina Schnorr von Carolsfeld, Anne Deinet, Ludwig Schnorr von Carolsfeld (the Tristan being in real life the husband of Isolde), Zottmayer, Mitterwurzer and Heinrich. The conductor was Hans von Bülow.

CHARACTERS

Tristan, *a Cornish knight, nephew to King Mark*	Tenor
King Mark, *of Cornwall*	Bass
Isolde, *an Irish princess*	Soprano
Kurwenal, *one of Tristan's retainers*	Baritone
Melot, *a courtier*	Tenor
Brangäne, *Isolde's attendant*	Soprano
A shepherd	Tenor
A sailor	Tenor
A helmsman	Baritone

Sailors, Knights, Esquires and Men-at-Arms

Time: Legendary

Place:

Act I – A ship at sea

Act II – Outside King Mark's palace in Cornwall

Act III – Tristan's castle in Kareol

Approx Act Lengths: Act I 80 min., Act II 76 min., Act III 78 min.

The earliest written record of the legend of Tristan seems to have been in the twelfth century. Wagner knew it from a thirteenth-century German version, although of course it dates from long before either of these sources: the story was a favourite with troubadours, who invented episodes with which to adorn the basic tale. Dante makes a bare mention of Tristan in the Fifth Canto of the *Inferno* and there is general agreement that one of the least satisfactory re-tellings of the legend occurs in Tennyson's *Idylls of the King.*

Wagner discarded accretions to the legend: indeed, he was at great pains to pare everything down to essentials, so that his final text makes passing reference to the tragic circumstances of Tristan's birth (his father was already dead and his mother died soon after) and to the deep sympathy amounting effectively to love which was roused in each of the central figures at the moment when Isolde spared the defenceless slayer of her betrothed; but leaves understanding of the strength of that sympathy to the music, which was certainly already taking shape in his mind.

The composer first mentions *Tristan* as a definite project in a letter to Liszt in late 1854, when he was writing the second act of *Die Walküre*, the second opera of his great cycle, *Der Ring des Nibelungen*. As a matter of history, he broke off *The Ring* after Act II of *Siegfried* in June 1857, not resuming until 1869. Ernest Newman has suggested that one reason for the interruption was an overpowering need to write music in considerable contrast to what he had been

Ludwig and Malvina Schnorr von Carolsfeld, the first Tristan and Isolde.

engaged on in connection with the Nibelung legend. Whatever the complicated reasons for the break, he wrote not only *Tristan* but *Meistersinger* as well between Acts II and III of *Siegfried*.

It is curious that he himself seems to have had an idea that *Tristan* with its small cast and, as he believed, simple staging would be a relatively easy undertaking for German theatres. In the event, the text was finished by mid-September 1857; the composition was well advanced by winter the same year; and he had finished the full orchestral score by early August 1859.

Before the action begins – if one can use so inappropriate a word of so action-free an opera – Tristan has in fair fight killed Morold, an Irish knight sent to extract tribute from King Mark of Cornwall,

and has himself received a poisoned wound. Only Isolde, Morold's betrothed, has the medical skills to heal him, but because he has killed Morold (whose body has been returned to her) she nurses bitter hatred for him. Under the name of Tantris, Tristan places himself in Isolde's care. But while he is lying sick and defenceless, Isolde discovers that a splinter found in Morold's wound fits a notch in Tantris's sword. She goes in to kill him, but is so affected by the look in his eyes that she cannot go through with her act of revenge.

Later, Tristan returns as emissary from the Cornish court and, regardless of the feeling that earlier passed between them, successfully asks the King of Ireland for Isolde's hand in marriage for his uncle, King Mark.

Act I in Peter Hall's production for Covent Garden with Pekka Nuotio (Tristan), Berit Lindholm (Isolde) and Josephine Veasey (Brangäne).

Act I. Tristan is escorting Isolde by ship to Cornwall. To Brangäne Isolde pours out her indignation at Tristan's procuring her for his old uncle. She is treated with scant respect by Kurwenal and finally decides that Brangäne shall administer to her and Tristan the death potion she carries in her medicine chest. Tristan realizes her intent, but Brangäne substitutes a love potion and, as the ship lands, the passion each has suppressed takes hold of them.

Act II. It is night and King Mark and his knights are hunting, while Isolde and Brangäne wait for Tristan to return alone. Isolde extinguishes a torch, the signal Tristan is waiting for. Their greeting is ecstatic and the duet is the centrepiece of the opera, interrupted when Melot escorts the King to discover the lovers together. Mark rejects the notion that Melot has acted altruistically, but asks Tristan how he, so loved and trusted, could be guilty of so great a betrayal. Tristan cannot explain what is beyond explanation. Challenged by Melot, Tristan drops his guard and is wounded.

Act III. Kurwenal has taken the wounded Tristan to safety in Kareol, sending word to Isolde. A

Berit Lindholm as Isolde in the Liebestod, Covent Garden.

An earlier view of Act I: Tristan confronts Isolde in a production at the Royal Opera House, Berlin, in 1907.

shepherd pipes as he keeps watch for the approach of a ship. Tristan in mounting anguish hallucinates that Isolde is about to arrive. Suddenly the shepherd changes his tune: Tristan senses Isolde's approach and tears the bandage from his wound, only to fall dead when she holds him in her arms. Mark arrives to find Tristan dead; Kurwenal killed in a despairing attack on Mark's own entourage; and Isolde about to expire on Tristan's body.

Wagner's opera is not a matter of words and music, of a dramatic action brought to the stage. Rather is it a musico-poetic idea remote from anything physical, a vast musical progression concerned with consuming love and a total need which excludes the outside world and all inessentials. When Tristan pledges himself and Isolde to the mystical other-world of Night, he insists that this is where he and Isolde belong: Night protects their love, while Day destroys it. It has parted him from Isolde and he senses that Day, when it arrives at the end of the second act – the only one effectively they spend together – will separate them for ever.

The drama – because, of course, there is drama – is enunciated in the prelude[1]: inextinguishable longing, an aching prolongation of ecstasy, a search for perfection which seems somehow to be less unattainable than accepted wisdom, here swept aside, knows to be the case. Act I puts forward the protagonists: Isolde, who cannot explain her forgiving behaviour to Tristan/Tantris unless through love; and Tristan, whose sense of honour forbids him to reveal why he had to return to claim her for another – a bride for King Mark might deprive him of his inheritance, but would bring internal peace in Cornwall. The intensity of their conflict sets in relief the inevitability of their all-involving love after drinking the potion. Act II

1. It is interesting that Wagner coined the word 'Liebestod' (Love's death), not to describe Isolde's last great utterance over Tristan's body, but for the prelude, using the word for concert performances he was giving in Paris in 1860. Originally, the opera's closing section, given in concert in conjunction with the prelude, was described as 'Verklärung' (transfiguration).

propounds the opposites of Night, where Tristan is at home, and Day, from which all evil flows, and does so with an incandescence found in perhaps no other music. King Mark is no cuckold, but a saddened, noble, mature figure, trying to understand the unfathomable, and enlightened only when Brangäne tells him in Act III of the love potion, by which time it is too late.

Act III propounds the most extreme, extraordinary and prolonged expression of obsession ever attempted in music. Tristan goes through the exquisite pain of frustration and maintains through all his hallucinations a vision of the ultimate ecstasy of fulfilment. Dramatically the scheme is simple: Tristan recovers consciousness to hear Kurwenal say he has sent to fetch Isolde, the only person with the power to heal his wound, and he latches on to this idea with a single-mindedness given only to the possessed. Three times the music reaches climax as he pushes his physical resistance to the limits; and after each climax he sinks into total exhaustion. Kurwenal despairingly wonders if his beloved master can survive another bout of such hysteria. Tristan inveighs against sun and light, symbols of Day; against the loss of father and mother before he could do anything for himself; above all, against the absence of Isolde. After his third collapse, his vision of Isolde is calmer and this time the music has an incomparable expressiveness: the passage begins 'Wie sie selig'.

The same scene in 1981 at Bayreuth in Jean-Pierre Ponnelle's production: Johanna Meier is Isolde.

Isolde arrives, Tristan dies. But at the end Isolde's quiet, lyrical outpouring of 'Mild und leise' is the one section of the work, apart from the prelude, known out of context. In this opera, it represents less the lyrical crown of the whole great edifice than emotion of a rarely paralleled order recollected not in tranquillity – nothing in *Tristan* is truly tranquil – but at least with all passion spent.

Tristan changed the course of musical history. The German musicologist Hans Redlich has written: 'The orchestral prelude alone, in which the implicit tonality of A minor is never so much as touched upon, is to all intents and purposes the first piece of practical atonalism, conceived half a century before Schoenberg and Busoni had drafted their first tentative experiments in the direction of a music of undefined tonality.' Generations of musicians and audiences have come to believe this to be true. Wagner *knew* it was true, according to Ernest Newman, but his conviction was sufficiently deep to allow him to leave the music of *Tristan* to speak for itself and all claims to be made by commentators rather than by the composer.

Tristan and Isolde after drinking the love potion in Act I – a romantic nineteenth-century painting.

RICHARD WAGNER

Die Meistersinger von Nürnberg

The Mastersingers of Nuremberg

Opera in three acts, words and music by Richard Wagner. Wagner had finished the text by the end of January 1862 and the score, after many interruptions, by late 1867. The première took place at the Court Theatre, Munich, on June 21, 1868 with Mathilde Mallinger, Sophie Dietz, Franz Nachbauer and Franz Betz. The conductor was Hans von Bülow.

CHARACTERS

The Mastersingers:

Hans Sachs, *cobbler*	Bass
Veit Pogner, *goldsmith*	Bass
Kunz Vogelgesang, *furrier*	Tenor
Konrad Nachtigall, *buckle-maker*	Bass
Sixtus Beckmesser, *town clerk*	Baritone
Fritz Kothner, *baker*	Bass
Balthasar Zorn, *pewterer*	Tenor
Ulrich Eisslinger, *grocer*	Tenor
Augustin Moser, *tailor*	Tenor
Hermann Ortel, *soap-boiler*	Bass
Hans Schwarz, *stocking-weaver*	Bass
Hans Foltz, *coppersmith*	Bass
Walther von Stolzing, *a knight*	Tenor
David, *apprentice to Hans Sachs*	Tenor
A night watchman	Bass
Eva, *Pogner's daughter*	Soprano
Magdalene, *Eva's companion*	Mezzo-soprano

Burghers, Journeymen, Apprentices and Girls.

Time: Mid-sixteenth century
Place: Nuremberg
Approx Act Lengths: Act I 82 min., Act II 57 min., Act III 118 min.

If the English have been inclined to pinpoint the Elizabethan era as an ideal, the Germans have had a tendency to make a cult of Nuremberg and medieval Germany. It was as natural for Wagner in the middle of the nineteenth century to light on Nuremberg, with its resonances of Dürer and Martin Luther, as a subject for a new opera, as it was nearly a century later for Benjamin Britten to choose for a

Friedrich Schorr, the most celebrated Hans Sachs of the inter-war years.

Lotte Lehmann as Eva early in her career.

Coronation opera the age of Queen Elizabeth I, with its overtones of new hope and an artistic golden age.

Nuremberg in the sixteenth century was a prosperous city of 30,000 inhabitants, famous for its physical beauty and its guilds. One of these was artistic, the so-called Mastersingers, who had set customs and complicated rules designed for the most part to keep out whomever the Masters did not want, but also to maintain and raise standards.

The leading Mastersingers were members of other guilds, craftsmen rather than merchants, and we see them 'on parade' in the opera's last scene, where they are the objects of Wagner's affection as well as of his mockery. It has been suggested that Wagner was presenting an idealised picture of a Germany dominated by its arts, crafts and customs at precisely the moment when the last remnants of that age were being swept away by the industrial revolution and its economic consequences; and that *Meistersinger* is therefore not only a monument to the old Germany but an exercise in nostalgia. Part of Wieland Wagner's work at Bayreuth as head and chief producer was directed, consciously or unconsciously, towards demolishing whatever

Norman Bailey sang Sachs in English in London and in German at Bayreuth.

pretensions his grandfather's work had in such areas.

Before the opera's action begins, we are to understand that Walther von Stolzing, a Franconian knight, has met and fallen in love with Eva, daughter of the rich, cosmopolitan goldsmith, Veit Pogner, who is also Grand Master of the Mastersingers. Since Pogner has made the decision that Eva's hand in marriage shall be the prize in the next day's singing competition, Walther must somehow contrive to be accepted as a member of the guild, whose rules are totally outside his previous experience, and from that position win the competition.

Act I.   In the Church of St. Katherine, it is clear that Eva returns Walther's interest. Magdalene sets David, her boyfriend and Hans Sachs's apprentice, to instruct him in the Mastersingers' rules. We meet the senior members of the guild. Beckmesser, the town clerk and a prospective (if improbable) suitor for Eva's hand, shows a spiteful turn of mind which is far from the detached and impersonal outlook demanded of his position as the guild's Marker, whose duty is to register faults in the singing trial. Pogner asks the Masters to meet a young knight of his acquaintance who wishes to become a Master. Walther is introduced (aria: 'Am stillen Herd', By silent hearth), but his Trial Song ('Fanget an', Now begin) breaks every rule. The Masters, led by Beckmesser, reject him. Only Hans Sachs finds his song novel and not without interest.

Act II.   That evening Hans Sachs muses at home in an aria known as the 'Fliedermonolog', but when Eva becomes impatient with his evasive answer about the singing trial, Walther suggests they elope together. The sound of the night watchman's horn is heard and Beckmesser chooses this moment to come a-wooing with his lute beneath Eva's window. Sachs contrives to frustrate both the elopement (by shining a lantern from his workshop) and the wooing (by singing lustily at his work). Beckmesser makes a bargain: if he may sing uninterrupted, Sachs can 'mark' mistakes on his shoemaker's last. The shoes are completed before the song, but David reacts furiously to what he thinks is someone serenading his Magdalene, attacks Beckmesser and rouses the neighbourhood,

so that the act ends in general brawling. Sachs offers Walther the hospitality of his house.

Act III.   In his room Sachs sings his 'Wahnmonolog', reflecting on the folly of the world and its inhabitants. He takes pleasure in writing out a song which Walther says came to him in a dream and pronounces it a work of genius. Beckmesser appears, limping from last night's beating, and sees the song in Sachs's handwriting on his desk. Sachs is willing to let Beckmesser try and sing the song at the competition and gives it to him. Eva listens enthralled while Walther sings a verse of his Prize Song and celebrates its inspiration by leading a quintet of exalted beauty ('Selig wie die Sonne', Blessed as the sun). The action now moves to an open meadow outside the city. The guilds enter, followed by the Mastersingers. Beckmesser makes a fool of himself with an inadvertent parody of the song Sachs allowed him to take away, but Walther wins general acclaim when he sings his Prize Song (aria: 'Morgenlich leuchtend', Morning was glowing). Eva rewards Walther's singing with a wreath, but when he impetuously refuses Pogner's offer of the Masters' chain, Sachs saves the situation with a peroration on the subject of art in general and German art in particular.

Wagner's illusion over *Meistersinger* was much as it had been over *Tristan*; that is, that any small German company could cast the opera well and should have little difficulty in mounting it. While it is fair to say that he wrote it for a normal orchestra with double woodwind, there the 'easy' nature of the work ends. It is otherwise built on a prodigious scale: it is of great length (longer even than either *Götterdämmerung* or *Parsifal*), it offers taxing roles for tenor and soprano (which Wagner throught relatively easy, as in comparison with Tristan and Isolde they probably are) and it contains in Sachs the greatest role for bass-baritone in opera, more demanding than Wotan from both a vocal and an interpretative point of view.

Die Meistersinger is above all a work about people and their motives. Let us start with Hans Sachs, the cobbler-poet and a hero figure in real life as well as in the opera. The role demands a singer of stature who is able to play the philosopher, the friend of the youthful Eva and the confidant of the knight from

Act I of Die Meistersinger *at Covent Garden in 1983: the set is designed by Barry Kay.*

out of town, as well as of the Grand Master of the guild. Above all, he must seem to be the idol of every apprentice and citizen in Nuremberg, so that when he makes his appearance for the singing contest, all rise to sing his praises. The singer must have every singing virtue: the power to dominate such scenes as the cobbling song of Act II and the final peroration; the legato to do justice to the 'Fliedermonolog' as well as to the later 'Wahnmonolog'; the clarity of diction for the opera's many crucial conversational passages; the humanity to involve an audience in the preoccupations of a long-ago city and way of life. A giant among basses!

Eva is a wholly sympathetic figure – youthful, impetuous, ardent, not throwing herself at her suitor but knowing her own mind. Her great opportunities come in Acts II and III: first in the scene where she tries to push Sachs into the position of Walther's unofficial champion and in her duet with Walther; and in the third act, when, dressed for the festival, she comes to Sachs's workshop ostensibly to have a pinching shoe eased, but really to find Walther, greeting him in a passionate outpouring of the greatest beauty and celebrating the birth of the Prize Song in the glorious quintet. When it is well sung, it is hard to believe that there is any more lovely ensemble in opera than this; and it crowns one of opera's greatest scenes, which has opened with Hans

Sachs's world-weariness, has given way to optimism at the dawn of midsummer's day and now ends with a burst of music of such beauty that one quite forgets that its combining of the strands of the drama qualifies it perfectly for opera's primary function of drama through music. As if to add a postscript to the role of Eva, her reaction to Walther's Prize Song is contained in a phrase of melting beauty which in itself would make the role worth singing.

Walther is a less interesting figure, but the challenge to the singer is considerable. In Act I, he sets out his stall, as it were, in an aria of real lyrical invention, 'Am stillen Herd', then caps it with his Trial Song, 'Fanget an', one of those wide-ranging tunes which sticks in the mind's ear long after something of squarer cut has disappeared. In Act II he distinguishes himself with a display of spleen which the circumstances do a lot to justify, but the last act shows him not only as a singer of stamina but, if the artist is up to the role, as a true lyrical master.

So good a character role is that of Beckmesser that only an artist of standing and resource will resist the temptation to go too far; and so good does the role still remain that, even when exaggerated, something will survive. Wagner's ability to parody his own melodies makes Beckmesser's attempted serenade (Benjamin Britten used to make out it was his favourite passage in the opera) and his botched wooing song into masterpieces of comic melody, but the century since Wagner has taken less kindly to his merciless mockery of Beckmesser-as-critic than he would have expected; and there have been attempts to make some kind of restitution to the sad figure of the disgraced town clerk by at least a gesture of forgiveness from Sachs before the opera's end.

In a way, Wagner was quite right about *Die Meistersinger*: apart from its length, it *is* an accessible work, highly rewarding to its audience, taxing but rich for its performers and a monument to the enduring qualities of German art which proves considerably less daunting in real life than its length might suggest.

GIUSEPPE VERDI

Rigoletto

Opera in three acts by Giuseppe Verdi; text by Francesco Maria Piave, after Victor Hugo's *Le Roi s'amuse*. Première at Teatro la Fenice, Venice on March 11, 1851 with Teresina Brambilla, Raffaelle Mirate and Felice Varesi (Verdi's original Macbeth) as Rigoletto.

CHARACTERS

The Duke of Mantua	Tenor
Rigoletto, *his jester, a hunchback*	Baritone
Count Ceprano, *Noble*	Bass
Count Monterone, *Noble*	Baritone
Sparafucile, *a professional assassin*	Bass
Matteo Borsa, *a courtier*	Tenor
Cavaliere Marullo, *a courtier*	Baritone
Countess Ceprano	Mezzo-soprano
Gilda, *daughter of Rigoletto*	Soprano
Giovanna, *her duenna*	Mezzo-soprano
Maddalena, *sister to Sparafucile*	Contralto

Courtiers, Nobles, Pages, Servants

Time: Sixteenth century
Place: Mantua
Approx Act Lengths: Act I 54 min., Act II 28 min., Act III 32 min.

The portrayal of a licentious and libertine court where the only character with moral fibre was the superficially corrupt jester and, against this background, plotting the assassination of an absolute ruler was always likely to cause trouble with the censors; and so it proved with both Victor Hugo's play and Verdi's opera. The play, *Le Roi s'amuse*, was given in Paris in 1832, but after a single performance it was proscribed and not seen again on the stage until 1882. The profligate ruler, it must be remembered, was originally not a fictitious Duke of Mantua, but François I, King of France. Verdi's opera was to be written for Venice, where the Austrian-appointed censor finally permitted its production, demanding first some minor changes in the libretto and a new setting.

The transfer to an Italian dukedom, with its overtones of the Gonzaga family, removed some of the political problems without losing the essence of the closed society, where one man's word was absolute and life could hang on a mere thread of approval: the rules, known to everyone, were subject to sudden change and only the demands of an overwhelming situation could break the mould. Such was a Renaissance court; nearer our own day, such could be the court of a dictator; and such the movies have shown us is the world of the Mafia, where the decision, even the whim, of the Capo is just as much law as was the fiat of a king in 1520. This was demonstrated in Jonathan Miller's successful production in 1983 for English National Opera in London, where the Duke and his henchmen ran the 'family' in 1950s style and Rigoletto was his barman and licensed joker.

Act I. The Duke is all-powerful and a womaniser (aria: 'Questa o quella', This one or that one) and he means to seduce a girl he has seen but whose name he does not even know. When Monterone, father of an earlier victim, demands satisfaction, Rigoletto is encouraged to mock him.

Left: *Enrico Caruso as the Duke, a role in which he was successful throughout his career.*

Right: *A poster published by Ricordi illustrating the cover of the piano score.*

Monterone invokes a father's curse — and the shaft goes home when we discover in the next scene that Rigoletto secretly has a daughter, Gilda, the apple of his eye whom he allows out of doors only to go to church. Before entering his house, Rigoletto is approached by Sparafucile, an assassin plying for hire whose services he rejects (aria: 'Pari siamo', We are alike). There is a tender duet for father and daughter before Rigoletto leaves the house again. The Duke bribes his way in: Gilda is his unknown beauty, but he pretends to be Gualtier Maldé, a poor student. Gilda seems receptive to his advances, but their scene together is interrupted and he leaves. To pay Rigoletto out for innumerable insults, a group of courtiers has planned the abduction of the young girl whom they presume is his mistress. The returning Rigoletto is tricked into helping them carry out this plan.

Act II. The Duke discovers that Gilda has disappeared (recitative and aria: 'Ella mi fu rapita', She was stolen from me) and is delighted when the courtiers reveal that they have abducted her for his pleasure. Rigoletto curses the courtiers for their evil deeds (aria: 'Cortigiani, vil razza, dannata', You courtiers, vile, accursed race). Gilda rushes for comfort to her father to the astonishment of the courtiers (aria: 'Tutte le feste al tempio', Every day in church; and duet: 'Piangi, fanciulla', Weep, my daughter). Monterone is seen on his way to execution and Rigoletto ends the act with a savage vow of revenge (duet: 'Si, vendetta', Yes, revenge!).

Act III. Rigoletto has engaged Sparafucile to kill an unknown man who will be lured by Sparafucile's sister to an inn. Before sending Gilda away, Rigoletto makes her watch the Duke (aria: 'La donna è mobile'[1], Woman is fickle) in an amorous

1. At Chambord, the vast castle François I planned and built on the Loire, legend has it that one of the window-panes carried a couplet in which he summed up his philosophy of life: 'Souvent femme varie/Bien fol qui s'y fie' (Woman changes often, Who trusts her is a fool).

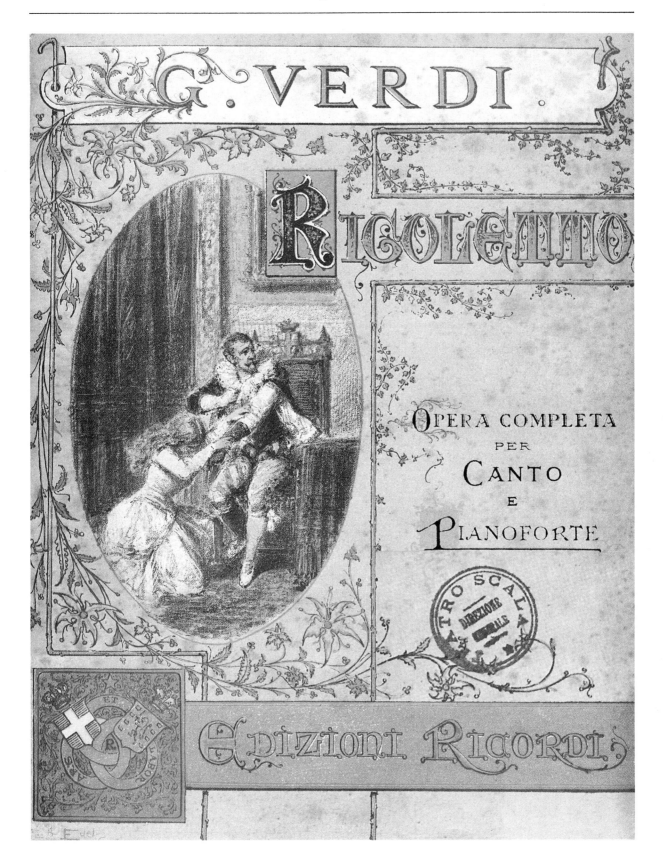

Rigoletto curses the courtiers in Act II (Ingvar Wixell in Zeffirelli's Covent Garden production).

scene with Maddalena, Sparafucile's sister (quartet: 'Bella figlia dell' amore', Fair daughter of love). Rigoletto then leaves. On her return, Gilda senses the Duke will be murdered and is determined to save him, so that, when Maddalena urges her brother to kill the first traveller to turn up at the inn instead of the Duke, Gilda falls a willing victim. When Rigoletto opens the sack in which the body is delivered to him, he sees his own daughter.

Audiences liked *Rigoletto* from the start, but the critics were less certain, finding it bewilderingly novel and lacking in invention − even, to quote the English critic, Chorley, 'Verdi's weakest opera'. The truth is that, after considering the subject several years earlier, Verdi was suddenly completely captivated by it for his Venetian commission. When it seemed likely there would be problems with the censor, he would discuss no alternative and moved heaven and earth to see that the text was passed without serious change. It was his most coherent and compact opera to date, written with such intense conviction that the first scene, for example, lasts less than twenty minutes but has, from start to finish, the feel of tightly coiled metal springing into life. In it Verdi establishes the court's elegant frivolity through what was for him the novel technique of comic opera: the musical texture is light and rapid in rhythm, the dramatic points being made essentially through contrast.

From the start, the figure of the Duke stands out as elegant and light-hearted, brilliant and sometimes febrile, and his major utterances range from the throw-away 'Questa o quella' with which he introduces himself; through the romantic fervour of his wooing in Rigoletto's garden and the tender beauty of his aria in Act II; to the climax of 'La donna è mobile' − a plebeian ditty of instant appeal and wholly fitted to character and surroundings − and the grandeur of his leading of the great quartet. Even in his wooing, whether of Countess Ceprano or

Gilda, there is an element of grace quite alien to some of Verdi's earlier tenors, whose breathing in such situations is decidedly heavy. Julian Budden suggests that the beauty and lyrical quality of the second act aria seem genuine for a quite simple reason: at that moment, the Duke is no monster but a spoilt child, to whom the fish that gets away will always be the biggest!

The central role is, of course, that of Rigoletto, the parasite who stage-manages the Duke's orgies and acts as gad-fly to the courtiers, but who in private life puts his daughter first and is above all a father, a position with which Verdi found it easy to identify. Verdi on his own created the modern Italian baritone: the voice is higher-based in his scores than in Rossini, Bellini or Donizetti (where the tessitura is nearer that of a Mozartian baritone, even what we now call a bass-baritone) and in this opera pitched more unremittingly high than in any other of Verdi's scores. As time went on, Verdi discovered more and more the full expressive possibilities of the Italian baritone voice: with 'Pari siamo' and the ferocious 'Cortigiani' he reached new heights of baritonal eloquence.

The solo numbers in *Rigoletto* represent dramatic climaxes, but throughout his career Verdi tended to move the emotional highpoints along in duets, in which related but often contrasted sections developed character and drama alike: in a letter he referred to *Rigoletto* as conceived in a series of duets rather than of arias. The relationship of father and daughter is shown in all three acts in duet: when the dying Gilda tries to comfort her father by blaming her murder on her own disobedience, she quotes her own words – 'Lassù in ciel', In heaven above – which have been the burden, constantly repeated, of her reaction to his first act agonising over the need to keep her away from the world which finally, through his unwitting agency, overwhelms her.

Gilda herself is sixteen years old. Verdi has caught

John Rawnsley and Arthur Davies in the first scene of Jonathan Miller's production, which made the Duke into a 'Capo' and Rigoletto his barman.

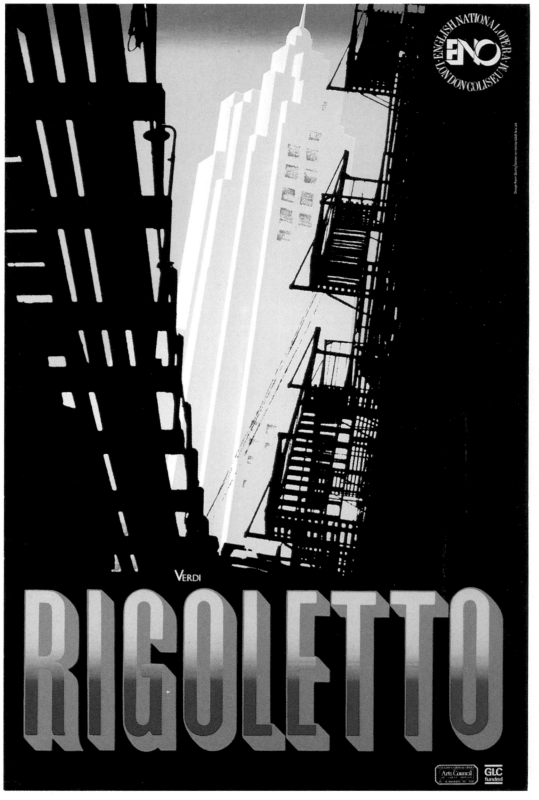

The poster for E.N.O.'s Rigoletto, *set in 'Little Italy'.*

'Duke' discovers that his gang has abducted Gilda for him (Act II in Jonathan Miller's production for English National Opera).

precisely the mixture of innocence and awareness of an awakening girl and wrote, referring to 'Caro nome', her aria in Act I: 'I don't see where agility comes into it' and 'At a moderate pace and sung *sotto voce* it shouldn't give the slightest difficulty'. In essence, of course, he is right, but the role has never been easy to cast without a soprano to whom at least some vocal agility comes easily. Contrariwise, a Gilda with too light a voice will have other problems, particularly in Act II.

For tenor and baritone, *Rigoletto* offers two of the prime roles of the Verdian repertory – musically the most elegant of all his tenor grandees, who must none the less possess the vocal quality of menace if he is to do dramatic justice to the role, and possibly the greatest, certainly the most taxing role of any Verdi wrote for baritone, with a demandingly high tessitura and a real need not only for power at

climaxes, but for the utmost clarity and beauty of timbre in the scenes with Gilda.

For all the splendour of its three major roles, *Rigoletto* is no mere offering to the canary-fancier, but a consistent dramatic achievement attained through music of enormous variety – the marvellously light-textured 'Zitti, zitti' chorus in the abduction scene; the unusual quality of the nocturnal music when Rigoletto and Sparafucile first meet; the wit, lightness of touch, even jocularity which constantly ornament the writing for Gilda, Maddalena, Sparafucile, Marullo, even Rigoletto and above all the Duke; and the unrivalled quartet in the last scene. In an even half-way decent performance, the listener oscillates between total seduction by the glorious melodic profusion and being swept away by the violence of the drama. It is a mixture that should never fail.

GIUSEPPE VERDI

Il trovatore

The Troubadour

Opera in four acts by Giuseppe Verdi; text by Salvatore Cammarano, after a play by Antonio Garcia Gutiérrez. Verdi encountered the subject early in 1850 and by April 1851 Cammarano had sent him a draft scenario. Verdi's mother died that summer and it was not until autumn that he returned to it. The libretto was almost finished when Cammarano died in July 1852. Legend has it that the music was composed between November 1 and 29, 1852: the première was in Rome on January 19, 1853 with Penco, Goggi, Baucardé, Guicciardi and Balderi.

CHARACTERS

Count di Luna, *a young nobleman*	Baritone
Ferrando, *captain of his guard*	Bass
Manrico, *supposed son to Azucena and a chieftain under Prince Urgel*	Tenor
Ruiz, *a soldier in Manrico's service*	Tenor
An Old Gipsy	Baritone
Doña Leonora, *lady-in-waiting to the Princess of Aragon*	Soprano
Inez, *confidante of Leonora*	Soprano
Azucena, *a gipsy woman from Biscay*	Mezzo-soprano

Followers of Count di Luna and of Manrico; Messenger, Gipsies, Soldiers, Nuns, A Gaoler.

Time: Fifteenth century
Place: Aragon and Biscay
Approx Act Lengths:
Act I 28 min., Act II 40 min., Act III 22 min., Act IV 40 min.

Spain is in the grip of civil war. Leonora is lady-in-waiting to the wife of the Prince of Aragon, in whose cause Count di Luna fights, while Manrico, the so-called gipsy, is enrolled among the insurgents led by Prince Urgel.

Act I. In the guard house of the Palace of Aliaferia, Ferrando tells how long ago, as the old Count's two children lay asleep, their nurse observed a gipsy woman gazing balefully at the younger. When the child fell ill, the Count had the gipsy burnt at the stake as a suspected witch. Her daughter pledged revenge; the Count's younger son disappeared – and a child's charred bones were found where the witch had been burnt. Ferrando would still recognise the murderous gipsy daughter, whose name was Azucena, if he saw her.

The scene changes to the Palace garden. Leonora waits to hear the voice of her admirer, whom she has loved since she crowned him victor in a tournament just before civil war broke out, but whose name she never learned (aria: 'Tacea la notte placida', The night was still and silent). The voice of di Luna, who is also in love with her, is heard, followed by that of the unknown troubadour. The rivals clash in a duel.

Act II.   Gipsies sing round a camp fire, into which Azucena gazes. The fire seems to mesmerise her (aria: 'Stride la vampa', The fire was blazing) and she mutters incoherently of throwing her own son into the fire by mistake and saving the Count's (aria: 'Condotta ell' era in ceppi', She was led away in chains). Her tale, half narrative, half vision, shocks Manrico, but she reminds him she has nursed him devotedly through the wounds he got in the recent battle: he must avenge her wrongs on di Luna's head. Manrico receives orders to take command of the recently captured castle of Castellor and learns that Leonora, believing him dead, plans that night to enter a convent. In the second scene of the act, di Luna waits in the cloister of the convent to abduct her (aria: 'Il balen del suo sorriso', The brilliance of her smile), but is thwarted by Manrico and his men.

Act III.   Di Luna is laying siege to Castellor when a gipsy is captured and recognised by Ferrando as the daughter of the gipsy they burnt long ago. The second scene is set inside the castle where Manrico and Leonora are waiting to be married (aria: 'Ah sì, ben mio', Ah yes, you're mine). When Manrico learns that Azucena is at that very minute on the way to be burnt at the stake, he leads his men in a sortie to save her (aria: 'Di quella pira', From that dread pyre).

Act IV.   Manrico has been captured and Leonora sings outside his prison (aria: 'D'amor sull' ali rosee', On the rosy wings of love). His voice joins hers, while monks intone in the distance in the famous 'Miserere'. Di Luna instructs that Manrico be executed and Azucena burnt, but countermands his orders when Leonora offers herself in exchange for Manrico's life (duet: 'Mira, d'acerbe lagrime', See how from bitter tears). The final scene is set in the dungeon where Manrico and Azucena are imprisoned. Azucena's mind is wandering and Manrico comforts her (duet: 'Ai nostri monti', Home to our mountains), but he turns on Leonora when she comes to release him and confesses the bargain she has made. Di Luna learns of Leonora's duplicity – she has taken poison to cheat him of his prize – and puts his earlier orders into effect, but, as

Ebe Stignani, a magnificent Azucena before and after the Second World War.

the axe falls on Manrico, Azucena tells him he has executed his own brother.

That *Il trovatore* has become a by-word for unintelligibility is due to two factors: Verdi wanted from his librettist dramatic situations, which he rated more highly than narrative clarity; and most of the complications of the original story were retained and compressed, with results that were nearly telegraphic in the terse way they told a convoluted story. The action-packed opera still holds the stage because those situations spurred Verdi to a display of

Maria Callas as Leonora.

musical energy and melody hard to match even in the uniformly vigorous middle period of this composer.

'For *Il trovatore* you need the four best voices in the world', Caruso once said. Without such voices, its robust demands will not be met. Without the technique to encompass its often florid music, singers will risk sounding like a herd of bulls in a china shop. The recipe is easier to quote than to put into practice, for in this case brains are no substitute for brawn and brawn is not sufficient without the technical skills often associated with less athletic challenges.

Many listeners start to wonder the moment Manrico sings off-stage what he will sound like in 'Di

Right: *Franco Corelli (Manrico) and Fiorenza Cossotto (Azucena) in the final scene at La Scala, Milan.*

Below: *Sandra Francis (Inez) and Natalia Rom (Leonora) with the nuns in Act II of Opera North's production in 1983, which was updated to the time of the Spanish Civil War.*

quella pira', which is not only the most famous and most spirited cabaletta in all Italian opera, but provides the climax of the third act with a top C. This is itself probably the most celebrated unscripted note in opera – Verdi did *not* write it, though it is certainly far from contradicting the music's spirit. But emphasis on the top C suggests neglect of the role's other demands. Quite as important as a stentorian top to the voice is a fluent delivery of the aria which precedes the cabaletta and which reflects the style of Manrico's earlier music; nor does anything supersede the need for long, mellifluous phrasing in the dungeon scene with Azucena and in the 'Miserere'.

Leonora is musically one of the most rewarding roles in opera, but also one of the most exacting. The arias of the first and last acts demand not only a wide range but phrasing on the broadest lines. Azucena is for the mezzo what Leonora is for the soprano; and while opera-goers love to talk about the 'Verdi mezzo' as a vocal type, they forget that the category is based on only three major roles – Azucena, Eboli and Amneris. These are Verdi's only substantial mezzo roles, with Ulrica in *Un ballo in maschera* as a lower-lying postscript to the whole story. Like Leonora, Azucena's range is wide, 'Stride la vampa' starting Act II as if the singer were trying to bottle up a secret she cannot share, and its sequel, 'Condotta ell' era in ceppi', forming a much more public confession, though still, with all its ambiguities, hardly an extrovert narrative. The first scene of Act III allows the singer a more straightforward expression of uncomplicated emotions as she defies her captors, but when we reach the famous duet in the last act, we are once more inside a mind which constantly topples over into a half-world of conflicting memories and emotions – at least, that is what the singer who is on top of the role should be trying to convey,.

Di Luna is a man of action, regularly thwarted in his ambitions – the only time Leonora is truly within his grasp, she is already dying – but a threat to all who oppose him. The singer who cannot dominate the first act trio ('Di geloso amor sprezzato') and make a thunderous climax with the cabaletta of Act II should not properly be asked to sing the role; but it is even more vital that he be equal to the smooth cantilena of 'Il balen', one of the most justly celebrated of all baritone arias, and the rapid bottom line of the last act duet with Leonora.

In *Il trovatore* codes of honour and chivalrous love, the force of arms and the fluctuating fortunes of war loom larger than subtleties of motive, second thoughts or tactical manoeuvring. They are put forward musically with an energy and directness which are vital to successful projection of the opera. Too much emphasis on any one of *Il trovatore*'s aspects will almost inevitably lead to neglect of another, so that what appears superficially to be one of the most straightforward works in the repertoire will once again have been short-changed in performance. It was once thought of as a bread-and-butter opera, a repertory staple and the source of more tunes for the barrel organ than any other, but in the late twentieth century, it has become a work not only for connoisseurs of singing but also for specialist singers. The rewards for everyone when it comes off are considerable.

GIUSEPPE VERDI

La traviata

The Fallen Woman

Opera in three acts by Giuseppe Verdi; text by Francesco Maria Piave, after the play *La Dame aux Camélias* by Alexandre Dumas *fils*. The première took place at Teatro la Fenice, Venice on March 6, 1853 with Fanny Salvini-Donatelli, Ludovico Graziani and Felice Varesi. The opera had little success, because the tenor was out of sorts, the baritone nearing the end of his career and the soprano, though a good singer, a lady of robust physique. Verdi made some revision, particularly in the baritone part, and forbade performances elsewhere. In May 1854 at another Venetian theatre, the San Benedetto, the opera was very well received with Maria Spezia as Violetta — young, pretty and frail, exactly the type Verdi was looking for.

CHARACTERS

Violetta Valéry, *a courtesan*	Soprano
Flora Bervoix, *her friend and fellow hostess*	Mezzo-soprano
Annina, *Violetta's maid*	Mezzo-soprano
Alfredo Germont, *a young man about town*	Tenor
Giorgio Germont, *his father*	Baritone
Gaston, Vicomte de Letorières, *Alfredo's friend*	Tenor
Baron Douphol, *Violetta's protector*	Baritone
Marquis d'Obigny, *friend of Flora*	Bass
Doctor Grenvil, *a physician*	Bass
Giuseppe, *Violetta's servant*	Tenor
Flora's servant	Bass

Ladies and Gentlemen, Friends of Violetta and Flora, Servants.

Time: 1847
Place: In and around Paris
Approx Act Lengths: Act I 29 min., Act II 62 min., Act III 30 min.

In January 1852 Verdi was invited to write an opera for Venice to be performed during the Carnival in 1853. There was a lengthy search for a subject and much discussion of singers, but it was not until November 1852 that Verdi and Piave agreed on *La Dame aux Camélias,* the play Alexandre Dumas *fils* derived from the novel he had published in 1848 and which, though completed by 1849, was not performed in Paris until 1852 because of censorship problems. Novel and play are closely related, but still different in their approach to their subject, and they constitute the younger Dumas's twin claims to fame. When he was only twenty, he had fallen in love with the brilliant Parisian courtesan Marie Duplessis, a girl from the country who was sufficiently intelligent and refined for her praises to be sung after her early death by everyone who had met her, including Liszt. 'Lola Montes could not make friends, Marie Duplessis could not make enemies' was one verdict, but Dumas broke with her

Claudia Muzio as Violetta.

when he found it impossible to accept not her love of luxury, which he could not afford, but the only way she knew of earning it. She was twenty-three when she died from tuberculosis in 1847.

The story of Marie Duplessis is progressively softened between the often harsh style of the novel, the more idealised presentation in the play and Verdi's treatment. By the time the opera came to be written, a vivid and touching slice of life had been transformed into something like myth – the myth of the 'fallen woman' who sacrifices all for love and is redeemed by her noble action.

For a time, legend had it that *La traviata* was a failure at its première because the audience would not accept so risqué a story in modern dress, but that is fiction. Verdi's original negotiations with La

Fenice stipulated contemporary dress, but for once he did not get his way. *La traviata* was played in 1853 in the costumes of 1700 and until well after the composer's death scores continued to specify that period.

Act I.   Violetta is giving a party at which she is introduced to Alfredo (duet, known as the Brindisi: 'Libiamo', Let us drink). There is dancing in the next room, but Violetta feels faint and only Alfredo stays behind to ask her how she is and to declare his love (duet: 'Un dì felice', Happy, one day). After Alfredo has gone, Violetta makes light of this declaration, but admits to herself the possibility that even she might fall in love ('Ah, fors'è lui', Perhaps it is he), then mocks herself for entertaining such a thought ('Sempre libera', Give me freedom). As she sings, she hears the voice of Alfredo outside.

Act II.   Violetta and Alfredo are living together in the country. Alfredo's happiness (recitative and aria: 'Lunge da lei per me non v'ha diletto', Away from her I can find no happiness) is disturbed when he discovers that Violetta is selling her possessions to pay their bills and he rushes off to Paris to raise money. Alfredo's father arrives to try to persuade Violetta to give up his son. She convinces him that she is no gold-digger, but gives in to his arguments that she must leave Alfredo if his sister's engagement is not to be broken off and her happiness blighted (duet: 'Ah, dite alla giovine', Go, tell the young girl). Germont leaves and Alfredo returns. Violetta protests her love to him, then slips away, leaving a note to say that she has gone to Paris. Alfredo is not comforted by his father's reminding him of the beauties of their home (aria: 'Di Provenza il mar, il suol', The sea and the earth of Provence) and dashes off to Paris.

The second scene of Act II is set at a party given by Flora Bervoix. Violetta is there in the company of Baron Douphol, whom Alfredo beats at cards. He publicly insults Violetta and is equally publicly berated by his father.

Act III.   Violetta, mortally ill, has heard from Germont that the Baron was wounded in a duel with Alfredo, who will come back to ask her forgiveness (aria: 'Addio del passato', Farewell from the past). Alfredo returns and they sing of a future together (duet: Parigi, o cara, noi lasceremo', We shall leave

Montserrat Caballe (Violetta) and Nicolai Gedda (Alfredo) in the Brindisi, Covent Garden, 1974.

Paris, my dearest), but, watched by Annina, Germont and the doctor, she dies in his arms.

The subject of *La traviata* must have seemed a bold one to its early audiences, but part of Verdi's daring was in abandoning, at least for a period, the great public events and gestures which had so far provided him with material and in accepting an intimate subject. The only direct precedent had been *Luisa Miller*, a purely private tragedy involving no public figures or events, and to some extent *Rigoletto*, in whose more intimate scenes Verdi mines something of the same vein.

For the unheroic, bourgeois world of *La traviata* Verdi had to find a new style. That he was successful is the more surprising since he wrote much of the music while still working on the strongly contrasted

score of *Il trovatore*. Piave started *Traviata*'s libretto in November 1852 and the première of *Trovatore* was in January 1853, but there is evidence that the composer had already mapped out some of the scenes and the themes that go with them. None the less, it is an incredible comment on these two densely packed, unremitting inspired scores that their first nights should have taken place within seven weeks of each other. Julian Budden[1] even refers to *Traviata* as the feminine counterpart of *Trovatore*!

To go with the new intimacy of his subject, Verdi evolved a greater flexibility of form. We meet it first in Act I when Alfredo's enquiry about Violetta's

1. Julian Budden: The Operas of Verdi (Cassell).

Maria Callas as Violetta arriving at Flora's party, La Scala, 1955.

health leads almost immediately to a declaration of love. Alfredo's 'Un di felice' starts shyly as he searches for the words he wants – there is nothing declamatory about this music – but once he has achieved his declaration, the banks of the pent-up flood burst in 'Di quell' amor' (This love of mine) and his verse ends with the words 'Croce e delizia al cor' (The torment and ecstasy in my heart). The climax of his declaration becomes musically symbolical of his and Violetta's love and is used throughout the opera, but those final words – 'Croce e delizia' – contain the essence of *La traviata*. The same conversational style informs the aria and cabaletta with which Violetta winds up the act, wonderfully expressive of the way in which Violetta, like Alfredo, is feeling her way at the start of the aria, but like him reaching certainty at 'A quell' amor'. In the cabaletta she seems to need to discharge the electricity which has been building up and she palpably celebrates the intoxication of dawning love at the same time as she denies its possibility. An aria of extraordinary potency!

In *La traviata*, as often before and after, Verdi employed the duet as a main vehicle of expression. This technique reaches its apex in the great scene in Act II when Germont comes to persuade Violetta that she must give up Alfredo. For all the grand passion between Violetta and Alfredo, this scene establishes the relationship of Violetta with her lover's father as the opera's most intense. From what seems at the outset likely to be a stern confrontation, we pass through Germont's perception of Violetta as no scarlet woman, his advocacy of the case for his daughter, Violetta's attempt to stem the tide of his argument, and her final yielding to her instinct for right as it forces her to make the greatest sacrifice she can imagine – giving up Alfredo for ever. Each short section has its own characteristic, whether strongly lyrical like Germont's 'Pura siccome un angelo' (Pure as an angel) or seeming to embody the ultimate emotions as in Violetta's 'Dite alla giovine', the centre-piece of the score as the scene is of the drama.

That *La traviata* belongs to a different world from that of Verdi's other operas is apparent from the very start: the prelude in no more than three minutes puts

Josephine Barstow as Violetta in Act I of John Copley's production for English National Opera.

Alfredo (Nicolai Gedda) insults Violetta (Montserrat Caballé) at Flora's party, Covent Garden, 1974.

forward a portrait of the heroine in two sections adumbrating successively her premonition of death and the confidence she initially feels in her youth and beauty. Later, the grand phrase of the second section takes on the passion of despair as she uses it to cling desperately to Alfredo's love. By the time of the prelude to the third act, we are in the presence of death itself, but there is no second section, no element of that life-enhancing quality which the opera's introduction so confidently asserted at the beginning of the evening.

The grace of the vocal writing, apparent throughout the work, derives, one may think, from the Verdi of the past, but the points that this writing succeeds in making aim unmistakably to the future – towards operas yet unwritten, by Puccini, Alban

Berg, Britten, Henze, by all who seek to make their dramatic points through music for the voice. *La traviata* is an extraordinary work which owes a great deal of its naturalness and the credibility of the dialogue to the original play, but is transformed by Verdi's score from a comment on the manners and morals of a particular period into one on life itself. After it was successfully revived, Verdi was asked which of his operas he considered to be his best and is said to have replied: 'Speaking as a professional, *Rigoletto*; speaking as an amateur, *Traviata*.' Not the least of the opera's virtues is that identification with some of the motives, predicaments and feelings of its characters is not hard for an audience to feel – and that turns us all, in the sense in which Verdi used the word, into amateurs.

GIUSEPPE VERDI

Aida

Opera in four acts by Giuseppe Verdi; text by Antonio Ghislanzoni from the French prose of Camille du Locle. The première took place in Cairo on December 24, 1871 with Pozzoni, Grossi, Mongini, Steller, Medini, Costa and Bottardi, conducted by Bottesini. It was first performed at la Scala, Milan on February 8, 1872 with Teresa Stolz, Maria Waldmann, Fancelli, Pandolfini and Maini, conducted by Verdi himself.

CHARACTERS

Aida, *Amneris's Ethiopian slave*	Soprano
Amneris, *daughter of the King of Egypt*	Mezzo-soprano
Amonasro, *King of Ethiopia, father of Aida*	Baritone
Radames, *Captain of the Egyptian Guard*	Tenor
Ramphis, *High Priest of Egypt*	Bass
The King of Egypt	Bass
Messenger	Tenor
A Priestess	Soprano

Priests, Soldiers, Ethiopian Slaves, Prisoners, Egyptians, etc.

Time: Epoch of the Pharaohs
Place: Memphis and Thebes
Approx Act Lengths:
Act I 42 min., Act II 40 min., Act III 32 min., Act IV 34 min.

Verdi hesitated some time before accepting the invitation of the Khedive of Egypt to write a piece specially for the new opera house in Cairo, whose opening was to coincide with that of the Suez Canal. Mariette Bey, a leading French Egyptologist, suggested the subject and provided a treatment which was turned into a prose libretto by Camille du Locle, a French admirer of Verdi's: this in turn was translated into Italian verse by Antonio Ghislanzoni. Large sums of money were expended on scenery and costumes, which were made in Paris but delayed there by the Franco-Prussian War. Verdi chose to keep to the spirit rather than the letter of his contract and the first performance at la Scala took place six weeks after the première in Cairo.

Before the action begins, it is useful to know that Egypt, dominated by a reactionary priesthood, and its neighbour Ethiopia were constantly at war and a recent punitive expedition by the Egyptians had resulted in the defeat of the Ethiopians. Among the prisoners is a young girl, Aida, who, unbeknown to the Egyptians, is the daughter of the Ethiopian king. Radames, a young Egyptian warrior, has fallen in love with her, but the king's daughter, Amneris, is herself in love with him.

Act I. Radames wonders if he might be chosen to lead the Egyptian army and rhapsodises about Aida (aria: 'Celeste Aida', Heavenly Aida). Amneris shows her jealousy of Aida. When a messenger brings news to the King of another invasion and it is announced that Radames has been appointed general, Aida joins in wishing him victory (aria: 'Ritorna vincitor!', Return as victor!), despite what this wish implies for the fate of her own people. The

Teresa Stolz, the first Aida in Italy.

Beniamino Gigli as Radames.

act's second scene takes place in the temple where Radames is invested with the panoply of leadership.

Act II.   Once again, the Egyptians have won. In her apartments Amneris is adorned by her slaves, before extracting from Aida by a trick an admission that she loves Radames. The second scene of the act is the famous Triumph Scene, in which the victorious army marches past the King and his court. Radames asks that, as a reward for his victory, the prisoners may be freed: Aida recognises her father among them. The crowd joins in the plea for clemency, but the priesthood secures the King's promise that Aida and her as yet unidentified father shall remain with them as hostages.

Act III.   Amneris, whose hand her father gave in marriage to Radames during the Triumph Scene, comes to the temple to pray. Outside, Aida waits for Radames (aria: 'O patria mia', O my native land), but she is first joined by her father who browbeats her into agreeing to discover from Radames the route his army will take when it attacks the Ethiopians. Aida at first seems to want Radames to

fly the country with her, then learns the secret of his route. Amonasro has overheard all. Amneris's sudden suspicious entry forces him to flee with Aida, but Radames gives himself up to the High Priest.

Act IV.   Amneris agonises before the trial of Radames for high treason, but is unable to persuade him to defend himself. To her outraged fury, he is condemned to death. In the final scene, he is bricked up alive in a tomb — but finds there Aida, who has come back to join him in death. They bid farewell to life (duet: 'O terra, addio', Farewell, world), while outside Amneris kneels in prayer.

There is little doubt that the subject of *Aida* was suggested to Verdi with some spectacle in mind; and when it was first performed at la Scala, we are told that there were over 300 people on stage during the Triumph Scene. Later performances and, for the most part, succeeding generations of audiences have almost entirely taken their cue from the Triumph Scene and seen the opera in terms of the trumpets and processions, the grandeur of the voices required to do justice to the score and the sheer bulk of

Above: *Sally Burgess (Amneris) and Wilhelmina Fernandez (Aida), Opera North, 1985: Philip Prowse's designs suggest the Egyptian Court of 1871.*

Below: *The Triumph Scene at Covent Garden with Paul Plishka (Ramphis), Montserrat Caballe (Aida), Robert Lloyd (the King) and Fiorenza Cossotto (Amneris).*

tradition which has grown up round the opera — camels, elephants, five hundred extras in the open air and so on. The reality is somewhat different and there is a case to be made for a slimmer view of *Aida*.

The prelude is concerned with Aida herself: the music is predominantly gentle and feminine, the counter-melody (representing the implacable priests of Isis) having a secondary position. The opening scene has Radames in audience with the High Priest, then in soliloquy and finally in a scene of private conflict (but public formality) with Amneris and Aida. The temple scene contains a dance of priestesses, but essentially the dedication of Radames to his role as commander of the army is a private scene, as is the long encounter in Amneris's private apartment between her and Aida. Act III is played out between Aida and her father, then between Aida and Radames: only the procession of Amneris to the temple brings anything resembling pageantry to the scene. The last act has Amneris face to face with Radames; Radames silent in front of his judges; and finally Radames joined in his tomb by Aida. As this brief analysis shows, only two scenes demand spectacle – the finale of the first scene of Act I and the Triumph Scene. All the same, the slimline *Aida* is a rarity, though I once saw something like it very successfully attempted at the vast Metropolitan Opera House in New York. But the public felt somehow let down and the production did not last in repertory.

Both the opera's geography and dramatic scale, then, to some degree contradict the idea of the monumental. On the other hand, tradition gains a certain support from the cut of the music itself. After the prelude, and apart from some of the music associated with Aida, the musical gesture is a large one. When Radames sings 'Celeste Aida', you are left in little doubt that he is warrior first and lover only second. The lyric soprano who can do justice to Aida's music is a rare bird indeed: in Italy the strongest voices are habitually cast in this role and that of Amneris. None the less, the performance which insistently denies the intimacy of the scenes for one, two or three characters will not do justice to the work.

And what an extraordinary opera it is, the quintessence of the grander side of Verdi's art and indeed of nineteenth-century Italian opera. If all the main characters are conceived on a large scale, Verdi skilfully makes them not only fully equal to their great public statements, but even more striking in their private reflections. Radames is splendidly shown as a warrior athlete in his soliloquy, his reception of the news of his preferment, the scene of dedication, the Triumph Scene and his confrontation with Amneris in Act IV. But he is more sympathetic, musically and dramatically, when in Act III he plots a future with Aida and later when, believing himself alone in the tomb, he finds Aida with him. Verdi's writing is here at its most lyrically persuasive, as it is almost throughout for Aida. Of course she needs the vocal muscle to dominate the top line of the great ensembles in Acts I and II; of course her two great arias are built on an ample scale; and of course there is an element of vocal (and dramatic) heroism in her defiance of Amneris in the first scene of Act II. But the listener is more likely to take away a memory of the end of the first act aria with its prayer for pity for her suffering or the insinuating melodies with which she tries to persuade Radames to abscond with her to the land of her birth.

Amneris is, perhaps, dramatically a more interesting study – the proud princess, easily roused to jealousy, whose love for Radames would undoubtedly strike us as touching if he would but return it. There is soft femininity in her repeated phrases early in Act II and at the start of Act III, while the tigress who rages against the priests in the last act is quickly transformed into the broken woman who mourns for Radames in his sealed tomb.

The role of Amonasro is much shorter than the other three, but his two scenes are extraordinarily vivid and he is put forward in music of power and beauty. Nothing could better demonstrate the warrior's pride than his Act II plea for mercy for the Ethiopian captives: nothing could be stronger than his denunciation of Aida when he believes (or pretends to believe) that she will not coax the secret of the military route from Radames. He clinches his ascendancy over Aida in one of the greatest phrases in all Verdian opera. The role is highly grateful to the singer and not at all uncharacteristic of Verdi's approach to writing for the baritone voice. But it is

The end of the Nile Scene in Jean-Pierre Ponnelle's production for Covent Garden in 1984 with Stefania Toczyska (Amneris), Paata Burchuladze (Ramphis) and Luciano Pavarotti (Radames).

also much easier to sing than any baritone role in his preceding operas and it marked for Verdi the start of a looser-limbed approach to writing for the baritone. This style can be seen on a larger scale in the music he wrote for Iago and Falstaff in his two remaining operas. It is not that these are easy roles, rather that Verdi still demands an extraordinary *musical* response from the singer but not quite the same aristocratic, traditional firmness of line. Like Amonasro, they are more declamatory, less *legato* in style than their predecessors.

As with most of the great composers of opera, one of Verdi's strengths lies in his ability to suggest a character from the moment the audience is aware of him or her. Aida is foreshadowed in the prelude and characterised as soon as she appears on stage; Amneris is a jealous, unhappy figure on her entry; Amonasro is a heroic fighter. Verdi's characters also have the ability to develop contradictions and softer

sides as we watch them grow. Aida is gentle by nature but also no shrinking violet – she has kept the secret of her parentage throughout her captivity. Only taunting makes her disclose her love for Radames, and she takes on heroic stature in her defiance of Amneris. Amneris, for her part, is a formidable figure in public, but considerably more sympathetic when she thinks no-one observes her: those melancholy, lovelorn phrases before she goes into the temple early in Act III would, if overheard, melt any heart not already given in love to someone else; and her mourning at the opera's close is as genuine as can be.

Aida is not, then, necessarily either an opera which wears its heart on its sleeve or whose characters do likewise. Rather, it is an Italian grand opera, whose secrets are disclosed in its intimate scenes and whose leading figures have worthwhile secrets to attempt to hide in public.

GIUSEPPE VERDI

Otello

Opera in four acts by Giuseppe Verdi; text by Arrigo Boito, after Shakespeare. The première took place at la Scala, Milan, on February 5, 1887 with Romilda Pantaleoni, Francesco Tamagno and Victor Maurel, conducted by Franco Faccio.

CHARACTERS

Otello, *Venetian general, a Moor*	Tenor
Iago, *his ensign*	Baritone
Cassio, *Otello's lieutenant*	Tenor
Roderigo, *a Venetian gentleman*	Tenor
Lodovico, *Venetian ambassador*	Bass
Montano, *Otello's predecessor as Commander in Cyprus*	Bass
A Herald	Baritone
Desdemona, *Otello's wife*	Soprano
Emilia, *Iago's wife, Desdemona's lady-in-waiting*	Mezzo-soprano

Venetian Soldiers and Sailors; Venetian Ladies and Gentlemen; Cypriot Men and Women

Time: End of fifteenth century
Place: Cyprus
Approx Act Lengths:
Act I 30 min., Act II 32 min., Act III 36 min., Act IV 32 min.

During their lengthy collaboration on *Otello*, Verdi and Boito (himself a composer of note) reduced a play of some 3,500 lines to an opera libretto of under 800, cutting the Venetian scenes entirely (though incorporating some of their material) and arranging the rest to flow with no break within the acts and only one change of scene (in Act III).

Act I. In Cyprus, people wait for the arrival out of the storm of the victorious Otello's ship: Otello steps proudly ashore and proclaims his victory ('Esultate', Rejoice!). Iago meanwhile plots with Roderigo (who loves Desdemona) and succeeds in making Cassio drunk (aria: 'Inaffia l'ugola', Come, have a drink), as he is resentful of Cassio's position as Otello's lieutenant. There is a fight, in which Montano is wounded, which is interrupted by Otello, who strips Cassio of his rank. Desdemona enters and the act ends with a love duet for her and Otello.

Act II. Iago advises Cassio to look for reinstatement through Desdemona's influence, then soliloquises on the glory of evil (aria: 'Credo in un dio crudel', I believe in a cruel god). There follows the first phase of Iago's planting of the seed of jealousy in Otello's mind, which is interrupted by a serenade to Desdemona by the people of the island and by Desdemona herself, who pleads Cassio's cause with Otello. This angers Otello and she offers to bind his head with a handkerchief, which Iago manages to steal. Under Iago's continued pressure, Otello's confidence evaporates (aria: 'Ora e per sempre, addio', Now and forever, farewell). Iago's account of a dream that Cassio has had (aria: 'Era la notte', It was night) leads to a joint oath of revenge (duet: 'Sì, pel ciel marmoreo giuro', Yes, I swear by the marble heaven).

Act III. The Venetian ambassadors are announced. Otello asks Desdemona for the handkerchief, is put off, and finishes by insulting her. Iago stations Otello behind a column to see Cassio play unwittingly with the handkerchief and the two plot Desdemona's death. The ambassadors enter and Otello's reception of them, his striking of Desdemona and a large-scale ensemble lead to Otello's frantic dismissal of the assembly. He lies prostrate, Iago triumphant over him, as the curtain falls.

Act IV.   In her bedroom Desdemona prepares for bed: her prayers are full of foreboding. Otello enters and strangles her. Emilia rouses the household and when Otello learns the truth, he kills himself.

The première of *Otello* was perhaps the most hyped in operatic history – at least, until that of Stravinsky's *The Rake's Progress* in 1951. Could the maestro, whose last stage work had been *Aida* sixteen years earlier, work the magic once again, this time in partnership with one of Italy's leading progressives, himself nearly thirty years younger? The almost universal verdict at the time was 'yes'; and while *Otello* duly went round the world, to New York within a year and London within two, its success with the public was a lot slower than with the critics. From the start, singers like Tamagno, Slezak and Zenatello revelled in the opportunities of the title role, but despite powerful advocacy by performers it has to a large extent remained caviare to the general; for it is a product of Verdi's last period, along with *Falstaff* and the late choral pieces *Quattro Pezzi Sacri*, a time when, however big the composer's heart, in the end his head ruled – to the acclaim of some and the disappointment of others. It is unquestionably a great opera, but, although written by the greatest composer of Italian opera, it belongs in another category from that usually signified by the description.

By the 1880s, Verdi was in his late seventies and an experienced composer. He was not inclined to change his style, to follow models from across the Alps and develop what he and his countrymen would have thought of as 'foreign' musical habits – 'Wagnerian' was the epithet attached to every new Italian work which seemed to its detractors not to follow the Italian tradition. But development, like pollution though less damagingly, hangs in the air

Victor Maurel, the original Iago, with the 73-year-old composer.

and affects a whole generation; and Verdi was not immune. So *Otello* maintains the inherited style he had used all his life, but it is used more incisively – more dramatically, if you like to look at it that way – than ever before.

Otello's first act is as urgent as the first scene of *Rigoletto*: we are in the middle of the drama from the onslaught of the first *fortissimo* chord. It is no surprise that Otello himself has no aria on his entrance, but rather an opening shout of 'Esultate!' which shows the warrior in all his glory, unhurried and without rival. We read of the clarion,

Above: *The Cypriot people celebrate Otello's victory in Peter Stein's production for Welsh National Opera.*

Left: *The first Otello, Francesco Tamagno, painted by Ferdinand von Keller (1889).*

Right: *Placido Domingo soliloquises as Otello in Act III.*

trumpet-like tones of Tamagno in early performances and have no reason to doubt these descriptions, but the fact is that the *tessitura* of the role is on the whole low, rising to the top of the tenor's register mostly at moments of stress (to a top C when he insults Desdemona). Few operatic roles are musically so precisely geared to the psychological states of the personality they depict.

Whenever he appears, Otello dominates the scene physically and morally (if not always tactically) and one of Verdi's planning problems was to provide resting places for even so strong and powerful a

tenor as it would take to tackle the role. Immediately after Otello's entrance, he provides the first of three such internal respites when, after a moment of victorious flag-waving, the people dance round a wood fire (a movement of remarkable vitality, considering it symbolises the restoration of confidence to the people of Cyprus). When Otello reappears, he is still the man of action, quelling the fighting ('Abbasso le spade', Put up your swords), but the arrival of Desdemona turns him into the man of imagination whose sense of poetry caused her to fall in love with him in the first place.

For the love duet Boito uses lines from the Senate Scene of Shakespeare's Act I and also from Othello's welcome to Desdemona in Cyprus. Verdi seizes the opportunity to write a duet in which, for the first time in any of his operas, there is no likelihood of dangerous interruption nor anything illicit in the passion the lovers feel for each other. It is a marvellous example of the long, quasi-conversational duets that Verdi wrote better than anyone else, and towards the end of the duet Otello embraces Desdemona to a musical phrase which is used prominently in the last scene of all ('Un bacio', A kiss).

Act II amounts to a battle of wits in which Iago plays Otello as a fisherman plays a salmon. The fluidity of the music exactly matches the dramatic process, so that we get to know Otello when he is perplexed and less certain of his line than when he has been presented as warrior or lover. Otello's second breathing-space comes when the people of the island come to serenade Desdemona. After it he is once more the man of action; his mind is made up and the act climaxes with an explosion of violence in the duet of revenge which he and Iago sing to pledge themselves to prove Desdemona's guilt.

When in Act III Otello meets Desdemona again, the ambassadors from Venice are already announced and the new situation – he now wholly believes in her guilt – brings out new music. Otello's despairing monologue, 'Dio! mi potevi scagliar' (God! You could have afflicted me), is more introverted than his previous music, drawing on all three of Otello's personas – warrior, lover and man perplexed. Respite comes when, in the ensemble after the entry of the Venetian envoys, Otello is

hardly required to sing, but in Act IV, once the violins have ended Desdemona's prayer on a high A flat and the double basses have heralded Otello's reappearance five octaves and a half below on a *pianissimo* bottom E, the opera's last movement begins. During it, Otello passes from the false calm of his entrance through the frenzy of the murder to his anguished remorse as he addresses the murdered Desdemona in the accents of the lover-warrior, while the orchestra remembers the end of the love duet and Otello dies beside the wife he loved 'not wisely but too well'.

There could be no greater contrast than between what Otello and Iago are required to sing. Iago is either bluff and matter-of-fact or (like Falstaff) all quirks and grace notes: he shows nothing in public between the honest ensign Otello believes him to be and the preening braggadocio he reveals to whatever audience he estimates as beneath him – Cassio, Roderigo and the Cypriot citizens. Verdi gives him brilliant tunes like his drinking song in Act I and bold, direct statements like his Credo (which itself contains some reversion to the lurching style of the previous act), but his music takes on a more insinuating character when he leads Otello into believing Desdemona false to him, culminating in his narration of Cassio's dream. In Act III, the man of quick wit and nimble tongue reaches his apogee in the trio with Cassio and the watching Otello, after which Iago, publicly thwarted of his ambition to succeed Otello as governor of Cyprus, has his greatest moment of ascendancy as he listens to the crowd acclaiming the general who is lying prostrate at his feet. In the opera's dénouement, as in Shakespeare, he hardly figures, but earlier he has established himself musically to such an extent that Verdi's original notion of calling the opera *Iago* seems credible.

Whatever her dramatic failings, musically Desdemona is no goose. We met her in the love duet, where, as throughout the opera, she is the ultimate lyrical heroine of Italian opera. Eventually she is caught in an impossible situation which she, who could cope with the disapproval of Venice in general and her father in particular over her marriage to Otello, cannot handle at all. In the quartet in the middle of Act II we hear her pleading with Otello from strength; and from weakness in the duet in Act III after he has inexplicably insulted her. Later in the same act, as she leads the ensemble, we sense from her melodic material both the depths of misery into which she has plunged and the inherent buoyancy which will make it possible for her to discuss with Emilia in the next act how all may soon be well between her and her obviously deranged husband.

Nothing in Italian opera is more beautiful than the great scene at the start of Act IV: the orchestra suggests the room's intimacy and Desdemona's Willow Song, a pathetic story of love betrayed long ago, ends with a 'good night' to Emilia which finally belies whatever confidence she may have summoned up earlier on. The musical cut of her prayer has a curiously modern ring to it: the text is first enunciated for several sentences on a single E flat, then rises through an octave and continues in a melody of great intensity, only to sink again to E flat. The final slow ascent to A flat above the stave collapses again to the E flat for a forlorn 'Amen'.

At the time of *Otello* Verdi was, by a long way, the most expert living composer of opera (as opposed to music drama) and the score is a model of operatic shaping, timing and invention. That it remains what one might call a 'festival' work — something to be planned and experienced only exceptionally — is a comment on its nature rather than its quality. It is just as much a part of the repertory as, for instance, *Don Giovanni* or *Tristan*, two other great operas equally challenging in their casting and their composers' ambitions.

GEORGES BIZET

Carmen

Opera in four acts by Georges Bizet; text by Henri Meilhac and
Ludovic Halévy, after the novel by Prosper Mérimée. The première
took place at the Opéra-Comique in Paris on March 3, 1875 with
Galli-Marié, Chapuy, Lhérie and Bouhy.

CHARACTERS

Dragoons
Don José, *a corporal*	Tenor
Zuniga, *a captain*	Bass
Morales, *a corporal*	Baritone
Micaela, *a peasant girl*	Soprano
Escamillo, *a bullfighter*	Baritone

Smugglers
El Dancairo	Tenor
El Remendado	Tenor

Gipsies
Carmen	Soprano
Frasquita	Soprano
Mercédès	Soprano

Innkeeper, Guide, Smugglers, Officers, Dragoons, Boys, Cigarette
Girls, Gipsies, etc.

Time: About 1820
Place: Seville
Approx Act Lengths:
Act I 48 min., Act II 45 min., Act III 40 min., Act IV 22 min.

For something like 150 years before the first night of *Carmen* in 1875, opéra-comique (the Paris theatre as well as the French genre) catered for a particular kind of family audience. For the most part, it had spoken dialogue between stretches of music and a happy ending. *Carmen* is substantially different, in that it is a serious story with a tragic ending, but quite a lot of the action was originally carried on in dialogue. Bizet died three months after the première, which was surrounded by controversy more to do with the subject matter than Bizet's treatment of it. There were 35 performances during the first season; the opera was performed in Vienna some six months after the Paris première; and when it was revived at the Opéra-Comique in early 1883,

it reached its one hundredth performance there by the end of the year – hardly the 'initial failure' of popular legend.

When the opera was due to be given in Vienna, it was thought helpful to have portions, but not quite all, of the dialogue set as recitative: Bizet's colleague, Ernest Guiraud (later responsible for 'doctoring' Offenbach's *Les Contes d'Hoffmann* before its première), did the job. This version was sufficiently

Above right: *Kiri Te Kanawa (Micaela) and Placido Domingo (Don José), Covent Garden, 1973.*

Below right: *The Toreador's Song at Covent Garden in 1973 with José van Dam as Escamillo.*

Emma Calvé, a high soprano whose Carmen was the most celebrated in her generation.

successful to be taken up for some 75 years in most of the large non-French opera houses in the world. It is a rather curious thought that the world's most often performed opera, which *Carmen* surely is, has achieved its popularity in a version which its own composer might have disowned! Not until the 1950s was there a move to return to Bizet's sparer, uninflated original with dialogue and no recitative.

Act I.   Soldiers mount guard in a public square near a cigarette factory, from which the workers emerge for a mid-morning break, Carmen among them (aria, known as the Habanera: 'L'amour est un oiseau rebelle', Love is a bird that's hard to tame). She catches Don José's eye, but he is unofficially engaged to Micaela, a girl from his native Navarre, who later brings messages from his mother (duet: 'Parle-moi de ma mère', Tell me about my mother). There is a fight inside the factory involving Carmen and Don José is sent by Zuniga to arrest her. She succeeds in persuading him to allow her to escape (aria, known as the Séguédille: 'Près des remparts de Séville', Near the ramparts of Seville).

Act II.   José has been demoted and imprisoned for his lapse. Zuniga and other officers are in Lillas Pastia's tavern, where they watch Carmen and her companions dancing (trio: 'Les tringles des sistres tintaient', The strings of the guitar were throbbing). Escamillo pays a visit to the tavern (aria, known as the Toreador Song: 'Votre toast je peux vous le rendre', I can respond to your toast) and is attracted to Carmen, but she is involved with a group of smugglers and is anyhow waiting for José, whose release she believes to be imminent. When he arrives, a love scene develops, but is interrupted when he tells her he must answer the bugle's call to return to barracks. She at first mocks him, but he makes it quite clear that he is in love with her (aria, known as the Flower Song: 'La fleur que tu m'avais jetée', The flower that you threw me). Zuniga returns inopportunely, is immobilised by the smugglers and José has no alternative, if he is not to lose Carmen, but to join the smugglers.

Act III.   In the mountains with the smugglers, Carmen reads her fortune in the cards: she foresees death (aria: 'En vain pour éviter', Useless to try to escape). José, already considerably disillusioned with the smugglers' life and conscious that Carmen is becoming indifferent to him, fights with Escamillo when he comes looking for Carmen and eventually leaves with Micaela (to the taunts of Carmen), who has come to tell him that back home his mother is dying.

Act IV.   Outside the bullring in Seville, Carmen embraces Escamillo before he goes in to fight. Left alone outside, Carmen is confronted by José, who kills her.

Prosper Mérimée's short novel is Don José's story, told by him while in prison under sentence of

A French lyric tenor whose Don José nevertheless won the highest praise was Edmond Clément.

death for the murder of Carmen. Bizet has changed the perspective so that Carmen is at least as much the centre of the story as José, with the irresistible attraction she has for José being the story's main driving force. His love becomes tragic when her shift of interest provokes a consuming jealousy. Various important clues to character are lost without the spoken dialogue: for instance, José reveals early in Act I that he joined the army because he had knifed a man in his home village and was fleeing from justice. Much of the dialogue is light, even bantering in tone – the music often takes its cue from the dialogue – but it hits harder than early family audiences can have expected: the dialogue makes it clear, for instance, that the girls who form part of the smugglers' band are expected to use their charms to keep the guards quiet at a much more basic level than that of mere flirtation – hence the disconcerting effect the opera had at the outset.

The opera's musical forms are concise and compact: almost no number lasts for more than five minutes, with the exception of the extended duet for José and the two-dimensional figure of Micaela, introduced into the opera as an innocent foil to the dangerous Carmen.

Bizet's music creates atmosphere very precisely. In the first act the public square is vividly recreated – the guard changing in front of the tobacco factory, half the world watching the other half passing by, everybody somehow expecting action to break out in the heat. The same goes for the after-hours, relaxed feel of the tawdry drinking-house in Act II, dominated at first by Spanish dance rhythms and later turning into a rendezvous for José and Carmen and for the change in José's destiny. Act III moves somewhat away from the world of realism: the smugglers as a group are more stylised – even romanticised – than characterised as individuals, but there is nothing unrealistic about the blaze of José's jealousy at the end. The legend that the best Spanish music is written by French composers perhaps started with the glitter of Bizet's recreation in Act IV of the Corrida. The music is full of anticipation though in the outcome it is Carmen's death at the end of the *faena*, not the bull's.

Bizet's instinct for musical colour seems unerring, his invention unremitting. He is not afraid to write arias for his principal characters which are operatic – for Don José, the Flower Song, the high-point of his plea to Carmen, is wrung from the heart; Escamillo's Toreador Song, immensely popular, has a rare swagger and confidence; Micaela's aria is a beautiful lyrical invention; and Carmen herself has strongly contrasted solo utterances. But Bizet's world is very far from that of grand opera and it contains more sophisticated gestures on a small scale than grand arias, large ensembles or rumbustious finales. His brilliantly crafted, subtly scored genre music moves the action this way and that and each number in succession seems not only appropriate in itself, but always contributes to the thrust of the whole opera.

It all sounds easy enough to mount and to cast, but does not always turn out that way. Micaela is straightforward enough, provided the singer is nothing less than a first-class lyric soprano. No good French-trained baritone or high bass seems to go wrong with Escamillo, but it is a rare singer of either category trained in a foreign discipline who hits the target firmly. Don José, not too hard a part to bring off dramatically, is difficult to sing, the first two acts demanding a strong lyric tenor, the third and fourth something a lot more dramatic.

But it is Carmen herself who gives the opera its colour and punch. Apart from the Habanera, with which she is introduced, and the overt drama of the last scene, she has nothing but a succession of songs to sing and an apparently foolproof character to play. None the less, the wholly successful Carmen is as rare in the role as the complete failure: something will emerge, but often less than you expect. Maria Callas, who recorded the role but never played it on stage, was once asked whether she thought Carmen was essentially a bad woman. She replied: 'Of course not, she is a gipsy. She thinks her destiny is preordained, that nothing can change it. Consequently she feels, "Why not act according to the impulse of the moment?" Carmen's only morality is never to pretend what she does not really feel. She is not calculating, but she *is* ruthless.'

MODEST PETROVICH MOUSSORGSKY

Boris Godounov

Opera in a prologue and four acts by Modest Moussorgsky; text by the composer from Pushkin's play and Karamzin's *History of the Russian State*. Moussorgsky was responsible for two substantially different versions of his most famous opera. (A) Seven scenes (Courtyard, Coronation, Pimen's Cell, Inn, Tsar's Apartments, St. Basil, Death) were composed and orchestrated between October 1868 and December 1869. When this version was rejected by the Imperial Theatre, Moussorgsky started on the opera we know today (B), finished by June 1872. Individual scenes were heard during 1872 and 1873, but the première of (B) took place on January 27/February 8, 1874 at St. Petersburg with Ivan Melnikov as Boris, conducted by Napravnik. The opera had considerable public success, but had disappeared from the repertory by 1882. In 1896 Rimsky-Korsakov revised and rescored the work, making a large number of cuts (C). Rimsky-Korsakov later made a more nearly complete edition (D) which was performed in 1908 and, with Chaliapin as Boris, made the opera widely known. (A) was heard at Sadler's Wells, London in 1935 in English. (B) has been heard with increasing frequency since 1945.

CHARACTERS

Boris Godounov	Bass
Fyodor, *his son*	Mezzo-soprano
Xenia, *his daughter*	Soprano
The Old Nurse	Contralto
Prince Shouisky	Tenor
Andrey Shchelkalov, *clerk of the Douma*	Baritone
Pimen, *monk and chronicler*	Bass
Grigory, *a monk; later the Pretender Dimitri*	Tenor
Marina Mnishek, *a Polish princess*	Soprano
Rangoni, *a Jesuit*	Bass
Varlaam, *renegade monk*	Bass
Missail, *renegade monk*	Tenor
The Hostess of the Inn	Mezzo-soprano
Nikitich (Michael), *constable*	Bass
A Police Officer	Baritone
The Simpleton	Tenor
Boyar Khrushchev	Baritone
Two Jesuits	Bass

Boyars, Guards, Soldiers, Officers, Poles, Pilgrims, People.

Time: 1598-1605
Place: Russia and Poland
Approx Act Lengths: Prologue 24 min., Act I 34 min.,
Act II 34 min., Act III 45 min., Act IV 50 min.

Boris Christoff's performance in the post-war years came closest to rivalling Chaliapin's.

Prologue. In the courtyard of the monastery of Novodevichy, near Moscow, peasants spurred on by a police official keep up a prayer for guidance. Shchelkalov tells them Boris has still not accepted the crown.

The prologue's second scene is set in a courtyard of the Kremlin in Moscow and depicts Boris's coronation. Boris prays for the guidance of his predecessor, Fyodor, the son of Ivan the Terrible, and that he will fulfil the trust placed in him by the people.

Act I. Boris has been on the throne for five years and is blamed for the famine and disaffection which are rife throughout Russia. In a cell in the monastery of Chudov, Pimen has almost finished his history of Russia. A young monk who shares his cell, Grigory, wakes up from a nightmare in which he dreams that he has fallen from the top of a high tower (historically, Dimitri, Fyodor's heir to the throne, was thrown from a tower and it was widely believed that Boris was the culprit). Pimen describes action in the army of Ivan the Terrible at the siege of Kazan and Grigory reacts to hearing that the murdered Tsarevich would, if alive, be about the same age as Grigory himself.

In an inn on the Lithuanian border two disreputable monks, Varlaam and Missail, are resting and drinking. Grigory is with them: he is wanted by the police due to an unguarded remark before he fled the monastery. Varlaam sings ferociously about his achievements at the siege of Kazan, while Grigory enquires from the hostess as to a safe route to the border. Police swarm into the inn. Grigory tricks them into thinking Varlaam is their man and escapes through the window.

Act II. In the Tsar's apartments in the Kremlin, his children play games with the Nurse, but Boris is overcome by cares of state and the weight of his conscience. When Shouisky is admitted, Boris accuses him of treason. Shouisky warns him of the danger if a pretender were to invade Russia posing as Dimitri, but Boris is at the end of his tether and collapses in hysteria at the thought of the murdered child.

Act III. In Poland, Marina Mnishek reveals her ambitions and also her subservience to the Jesuit Rangoni. The false Dimitri (Grigory) is in love with

Fyodor Chaliapin's mesmeric performance brought Boris Godounov *to the world's attention.*

her and she stimulates his resolve to lead an army on Moscow.

Act IV. The Douma in session discusses measures to repel the invasion from Poland, but the Tsar enters, plainly in the grip of terror. After Pimen describes how a blind shepherd received his sight at the tomb of the murdered Tsarevich, Boris collapses, then sends for his son and dies.

In the forest of Kromy, lynch law grips the mob, children mock a Simpleton and Dimitri at the head of his army bids the crowd follow him to Moscow. Only the Simpleton stays, lamenting the fate of the Russian people.

The old joke about Russian music, opera in particular, is that on the whole it was written by somebody other than the composer and that it takes as long to decide what version to perform as it does to rehearse whatever is selected. Where *Boris* is concerned, current perception would opt for Moussorgsky's (B) (or conceivably (A)), accepting its dark colours and sometimes awkward orchestration as representing the true concept of a composer whose vision may have been a little blurred but was invariably powerful. Rimsky-Korsakov's scoring is more obviously brilliant and sometimes makes points which Moussorgsky may have intended, but which can go for nothing in other than a revelatory performance of (A) or (B). I have heard it argued by a conductor who has performed both versions that Moussorgsky's can be achieved only under festival conditions and that Rimsky-Korsakov's is better suited to the circumstances of repertory performance and to the needs of a repertory audience.

The Polish Act was added by Moussorgsky on the advice of his friends when the Imperial Theatre rejected (A). The intention was to provide contrast to the dark events of his original, but the effect, hindsight might conclude, has been to turn dramatic tautness into a more loosely-knit chronicle. The act contains some attractive music and concludes with what may be the most famous tune Moussorgsky ever wrote, but the price paid for its inclusion is a heavy one.

The question of a version contains another problem. In (A), at the start of Act IV, there occurs a scene outside the Church of St. Basil where the grumbling populace waits for the service to finish in order to supplicate the Tsar for alms. A poor

Georges Wakhevich's design for Act II, Covent Garden, 1948.

The Douma in the production from the Kirov Theatre, Leningrad.

Simpleton pathetically bewails the fate of Russia and some urchins by a trick steal his few kopeks. When Boris comes from the church, the Simpleton asks him to punish the children for their cruelty – as once upon a time he killed the young Tsarevich. Boris quells the consternation this produces in his entourage and asks the Simpleton as a man touched by God to pray for him. The Simpleton refuses, saying it would be like praying for Herod. The scene is highly rated by singers of the title role because it shows the Tsar in magnanimous light, but it does not figure in (B) (nor in (C) or (D), of course); and for (B), Moussorgsky re-positioned the Simpleton's music in the forest of Kromy. To include *both* scenes involves a solecism, as each demands the Simpleton's song if it is to finish properly and to have the song dominate two scenes is to invest it with more significance than the composer meant it to bear.

Even a decision about St. Basil does not bring us to the end of the problem of version. Moussorgsky's (A) ended with the death of the Tsar, but in (B), advised again (it is said) by friends, he placed the scene of Boris's · death *before* the so-called revolutionary scene, thus implicitly making the Russian people the true protagonists of his drama. In the right production, this can produce an appropriately cathartic effect – as it did in Peter Brook's staging at Covent Garden in 1948 – but it remains hard to follow Boris's death scene without a serious risk of anti-climax.

There is no better opportunity for a bass-baritone who is also a fine actor than the role of Boris. Once upon a time the opera was enjoyed mainly because of these opportunities and the way a Chaliapin or a Christoff would take them. We meet him in introspective mood as he prays for help before his coronation, but Act II shows him with all his defences down. With his son, he pours out his agony of mind in a grandiose monologue, but reveals even more of himself in the great confrontation with Prince Shouisky. This starts with vigorous accusations of treason and double-dealing, which Shouisky brushes aside as slander; he maintained

The Icon door closes to isolate the dying Boris from the world: Covent Garden, 1948.

and Shouisky makes a show of soothing his fears. When figures on a chiming clock revolve, Boris sees in them an apparition of the murdered child, so that his hysteria takes on the colour of madness and he prays to God for forgiveness – a scene of remarkable power.

The climax of the title role comes with the death scene, when Boris is left alone with his son, to whom he bids farewell, assuring him that he is the lawful heir to the throne of Russia. He prays simply and movingly to God, then sinks down as the passing bell is heard and the chant of the monks praying for his soul. The music becomes simpler as the Tsar's strength ebbs; as he sinks, he seems hardly able to manoeuvre his voice up or down.

Boris Godounov is far from being a matter of the title role alone. It is full of opportunities for other singers – fine roles for two other basses (Varlaam's ferocious song about his achievements as a soldier at Kazan is a magnificent affair; and Pimen is one of the grandest roles in the 'high priest' category); tenor and mezzo have striking music to sing; the Simpleton is a memorable inspiration; and even the short solo for Shchelkalov in the opening scene is impressive in its gravity. The writing throughout is graphic, whether Moussorgsky is writing short solos for the children in the Tsar's apartments; providing the chorus with opportunities as peasants outside the monastery, while waiting for the coronation, or in the forest of Kromy; or in Pimen's cell suggesting the slow and laborious action of writing. Its early detractors claimed that *Boris* was no more than a loosely connected series of historical scenes, adding up to less than the opera's title suggested. But time has demonstrated the score's extraordinary overall richness and most audiences would agree that there is no greater epic in all opera.

lines of communication with the rebels in order to report on their movements – there could be Russians attracted to a pretender's cause if he were to cross the border as Dimitri. Boris orders Shouisky to confirm that it was Dimitri's body buried at Uglich

PETER ILITSCH TCHAIKOVSKY

Yevgeny Onyegin

Eugene Onegin

Opera in three acts by Peter Ilitsch Tchaikovsky; text by the composer and K. S. Shilovsky, after Pushkin. The première took place at the Moscow Conservatoire on March 29, 1879 with a student cast.

CHARACTERS

Madame Larina, *a widow with an estate*	Mezzo-soprano

Her daughters

Tatiana	Soprano
Olga	Contralto

Filipievna, *Tatiana's old nurse*	Mezzo-soprano
Lenski, *Olga's fiancé*	Tenor
Eugene Onegin, *his friend*	Baritone
Prince Gremin, *a retired general*	Bass
A Captain	Bass
Zaretski	Bass
Monsieur Triquet, *a Frenchman*	Tenor

Peasants, Party Guests

Time: Late eighteenth century
Place: Madame Larina's estate; St. Petersburg
Approx Act Lengths: Act I 76 min., Act II 42 min., Act III 36 min.

Act I.   In her garden Madame Larina and her family are engaged in the summer pursuits of a country house when Lenski and Onegin pay a social call. At the end of the visit, Filipievna wonders if Tatiana could be interested in Onegin.

That night, in her bedroom, Tatiana writes to tell Onegin that she is in love with him. Next day, in the garden, Onegin tells Tatiana that love and marriage are not for him.

Act II.   During a dance for Tatiana's birthday, Onegin flirts with Olga and Lenski, to whom she is engaged, demands satisfaction. Next morning, they fail to make it up and Lenski is killed in the duel.

Act III.   Duelling was illegal in Russia (though Pushkin himself was killed in one six years after writing *Yevgeny Onyegin*) and Onegin has spent several years abroad after the death of Lenski. At a fashionable ball in St. Petersburg, he discovers his middle-aged cousin, Prince Gremin, is married to Tatiana, with whom he now feels himself passionately in love.

Later, at her house, Tatiana, confronted not only by a distraught Onegin but by the certainty that she returns his love, with difficulty summons the strength to rebuff him.

Yevgeny Onyegin was the fifth of Tchaikovsky's ten operas, a healthy total to set against the notion that he was at home primarily in instrumental forms and wrote for the stage as a sideline. Both *Onyegin* and *The Queen of Spades*, his two most popular works in the form, are based on poems by Pushkin, but Tchaikovsky, like many other composers, often seems to have had difficulty finding the right libretto to fire his imagination and set him off on the right path.

Not so with *Onyegin*, which was suggested to him as a subject in 1877 and over which he hesitated only for fear he might be accused of misrepresenting a classic – so highly was Pushkin's dramatic poem already regarded. Once his mind was made up, he seized on the episode of the letter and composed that scene first, writing at the time that he loved Tatiana and was terribly indignant with Onegin, who seemed to him a cold, heartless coxcomb. So strong was his identification with the heroine's dilemma that, when he got a letter from a girl at the Conservatoire in Moscow saying that she was in love with him, he made up his mind at all costs not to emulate Onegin: though he was homosexual by nature, he embarked on a loveless marriage, from which he was lucky to escape with nothing worse than a nervous breakdown before the doctors insisted the marriage come to an end.

The libretto follows fairly closely the lines of the poem, apart from throwing emphasis on Tatiana rather than Onegin, but much of Pushkin's social commentary finds no place in it: the girls in the last scene of Act I, for instance, sing to provide the scene with a pastoral background, whereas in Pushkin their singing is on the overseer's instructions, in order that they cannot pop the fruit they are picking into their mouths.

The conclusion of the Letter Scene in the production from the Kirov Opera, Leningrad.

Onegin and Gremin meet: Ileana Cotrubas (Tatiana), Gwynne Howell (Gremin) and Victor Braun (Onegin) in Peter Hall's production at Covent Garden.

In those of his operas which have specifically Russian and non-heroic themes, Tchaikovsky took pains to establish by musical means a strongly characterised social scene and atmosphere: this is very apparent in *Onyegin*. Madame Larina and Filipievna are making jam as the curtain rises – the lady of the house engaged in the more gentle side of the work – and the girls Tatiana and Olga practise a duet indoors: a quartet thus develops quite naturally and without straining the dramatic situation. The nature of the solo utterances in this opening scene is lyrical and intimate, as is appropriate in an opera whose characters have a tendency to be life-like, rather than romantic giants. Estate workers sing attractive pieces here, and again in the third scene of the act while picking raspberries; and there is much skill in the way the composer pins down the social conventions of Madame Larina's unpretentious country dance in Act II, with its admirable waltz, and contrasts it with the grand St. Petersburg ball of the last act, very much a 'white tie' affair as compared with the other's essentially 'black tie' accent.

Tchaikovsky was particularly good at developing a scene on the musical basis of a dance: he would set conversation, little solos for different characters, fluctuating dramatic tensions, all against a great set piece in dance form. Its rhythms provided impetus while allowing the dramatic situation to rise and fall quite naturally before bringing the whole thing to a climax, with a change of tempo to match the evolved dramatic situation. The opening scenes of both Acts II and III in their different ways are developed with considerable acumen in precisely this way; and it is interesting that Prokofiev in the second scene of his *War and Peace* contrived something not dissimilar over sixty years later for the meeting of Natasha and Andrei at her first ball.

The main characters have beautiful solos – Prince Gremin's in the last act is almost his only utterance, but establishes him immediately as no lay figure but a thinking, feeling person; and Lenski, after rapturous *arioso* music earlier on, has two moments of great lyrical import. In the climax of Act II's dance he recalls in music of melting tenderness the happiness he associates with Madame Larina's house, which he has now made the scene of a scandal; and before the duel, his fine lyrical farewell to the life he has loved so well but for so short a time is supreme amongst tenor scenes in Russian opera. With Onegin the composer obviously found it more difficult to sympathise, but he writes music for him in the first two acts which is at the same time rather cold and yet youthful, before allowing in the third act full rein to the romantic, Byronic personality so far dormant, even permitting him to quote (transposed down a minor third) a section of Tatiana's Letter Scene.

Tatiana is, of course, the central figure, her music growing outwards from the episode of the letter and the other characters are somehow always seen in relation to her even if their music is not derived directly from hers. The scene where she first prepares for bed, then writes impulsively to Onegin is a remarkable affair. The musical introduction is derived from the opera's prelude, itself intimately concerned with Tatiana, and the moment Filipievna leaves and she is alone, the overwhelming nature of her feelings finds expression in the orchestra, until she releases her pent-up emotions in a great up-beat phrase like a huge intake of breath, her mind made up to take the plunge. This is only a prelude to an outpouring of young love not equalled elsewhere in opera, full of the doubts and self-torment that Tchaikovsky understood too well. The orchestra suggests the act of writing, dropping fourths and fifths crossing a simple melodic line in the oboe, and its wealth of detail implies what she does not say aloud. The mood is conversational, fragmentary: snatches of recitative are interspersed with the letter writing, making the music sometimes lyrical and

Dimitri Smirnoff, pre-revolutionary Russia's outstanding lyric tenor, as Lenski.

Galina Vishnevskaya at Tatiana.

reflective, sometimes impassioned and almost declamatory, until Tatiana declares that everything she has ever done has been for *him*, the horn's reaction seeming to give assent to her declaration.

The pathos embodied in the slow, lilting waltz in D flat to which Tatiana and her husband make their entrance at the St. Petersburg ball is closely associated with her personality. In the last scene of all – an extended duet in several sections – the mixture of hurt and dignity with which she remembers the pain of rejection so many years ago leads to grand, sweeping music in which she admits to Onegin that she returns his love, but then admonishes him to remember the path of honour and leave her.

Though written in the same decade as *Boris* the lyrical scale on which *Yevgeny Onyegin* is conceived, with its domestic references and gentle, unheroic overtones, could hardly be in greater contrast with that opera's epic grandeur, yet to Russians it is no less typical of their national music.

Pavel Khokhlov, who sang the title role in the professional première of the opera at the Bolshoi Theatre, Moscow, in 1881.

PIETRO MASCAGNI

Cavalleria Rusticana

Rustic Chivalry

Opera in one act by Pietro Mascagni; text by G. Menasci and G. Targioni-Tozzetti, after a story by Giovanni Verga. The première took place at Teatro Costanzi, Rome on May 17, 1890 with Gemma Bellincioni and Roberto Stagno, conducted by Leopoldo Mugnone.

CHARACTERS

Turiddu, *a young soldier*	Tenor
Alfio, *the village teamster*	Baritone
Lola, *his wife*	Mezzo-soprano
Mamma Lucia, *Turiddu's mother*	Contralto
Santuzza, *a village girl*	Soprano

Villagers, Peasants, Boys

Time: 'The present', on Easter Day
Place: A village in Sicily
Approx Length: 70 min.

In the 1954 edition of Grove's Dictionary *verismo* is 'a term used to classify Italian opera of a sensational, supposedly "realistic" kind, including the works of Mascagni, Leoncavallo, Puccini, Giordano etc.' Other works of reference (including the New Grove, 1980), less tendentiously, allow that the essential difference between *verismo* operas and their predecessors lies in the libretti, which deal with everyday situations, as opposed to costume plays, historical episodes or legends.

Whatever definition is attempted, the average opera-goer understands from the word a distinct comment on the music and expects something demanding first and foremost power and attack from the singer and only secondarily a smooth *legato* or much relevance to the art of *bel canto*. This is very far from being the whole truth: interestingly, the great tenor Fernando de Lucia, renowned for the *bel canto* style demonstrated in his gramophone recordings, was the first tenor at Covent Garden to sing both *Cavalleria Rusticana* and *Pagliacci*, the

first in 1892 with Emma Calvé and the second with Melba in 1893 – and the two sopranos were themselves pupils of Mathilde Marchesi, a great teacher of the *bel canto* school.

Cavalleria Rusticana was originally a short story by Giovanni Verga, which as a stage play gave Eleonora Duse one of her first great successes. The story is considerably different in manner from the opera, at once earthier (Alfio blinds Turiddu with dust before fatally wounding him) and more dispassionate in tone. The opera's motivation, it seems to me, is not only tragic but steeped in the ritual of a primitive, believing people. Turiddu knows that, if Alfio challenges him (as he must), he cannot refuse to fight; and he knows that in justice he will be killed. By comparison, *Pagliacci*, with which *Cavalleria* is usually teamed, is highly effective, but in terms of a newspaper anecdote of a *crime passionel* rather than of tragedy.

During the prelude, the voice of Turiddu is heard singing a serenade to Lola, Alfio's wife (aria, known

The Easter Hymn at Covent Garden, designed and produced by Franco Zeffirelli.

as the Siciliana: 'O Lola'). Turiddu had fallen in love with Lola, the village belle, before he went off for military service: Lola did not wait for him and married Alfio. Turiddu returned and had an affair with Santuzza, who is now pregnant, but he has not given up hope of Lola.

The curtain rises on villagers going about their business on Easter morning. Mamma Lucia tells Santuzza that Turiddu has gone off to fetch wine, something Santuzza knows to be false as she saw him that morning in the village. Alfio makes his entrance (aria: 'Il cavallo scalpita', My horse is stamping), asks for wine and, when he is told that Turiddu has gone to fetch more, confirms Santuzza's story. The Easter Hymn rings out and Santuzza tells Mamma Lucia the sad story of her seduction by Turiddu and his continued preference for Lola (aria: 'Voi lo sapete, O mamma', You know the story, mother).

Turiddu appears and Santuzza accuses him of hanging about Lola's house. At that moment, Lola appears on her way to church. Santuzza begs Turiddu to stay with her, but he follows Lola. Santuzza denounces Turiddu and Lola to Alfio, who vows revenge. The famous intermezzo denotes the passage of time before Turiddu offers wine to the people coming out of church. Alfio refuses and challenges him to a fight. Turiddu bids a heart-felt farewell to his mother, asks her to look after Santuzza if anything were to happen to him and goes to meet Alfio. A moment later, the cry goes up that he has been killed.

I cannot but think it unfortunate that the *verismo* school is often thought to have started with *Cavalleria*, whose subject is sensational in that it deals with a contemporary story, but whose composer at that time wrote as an instinctive successor to Bellini. In the first stage of his career, a period which also embraces *L'amico Fritz*, Mascagni wrote a lyrical and highly expressive vocal line and only occasionally in *Cavalleria* (notably in Alfio's entrance song and the duet for him and Santuzza) is the score touched by the vigour we have come in an

Bellincioni and Stagno, Cavalleria rusticana*'s original principals.*

over-simplified way to think of as 'veristic'.

A lyrical mood is set in the prelude, Turiddu's yearning, long-breathed Siciliana setting the tone for what he sings later – the vehement but linear-based music of the duet with Santuzza; the brilliant drinking song ('Viva il vino spumeggiante', Long live the sparkling wine) in which he toasts the villagers; or his heart-felt, Puccinian farewell to his mother ('Mamma, quel vino è generoso', Mother, this wine is strong). The choruses which bring the village to life at the start of the opera and the Easter Hymn are just as melodic. Santuzza, after a beautiful aria in which she explains her situation to Mamma Lucia, reaches her high point in the confrontation with Turiddu outside the church, a scene of great drama but, with its long pleading line, musically impressive as well. More positively inventive is the passage beginning 'Turiddu mi tolse l'onore' (Turiddu tore my honour from me), marvellously taut and anguished and leading inevitably to a furious explosion from Alfio which is tantamount to a death sentence on Turiddu, however much Santuzza may inwardly regret it.

The intermezzo, once a constituent part of every popular programme for orchestra, tea band or cinema organ, is today less often heard on its own. Nevertheless, its lyrical expressiveness and direct appeal, when heard in context, will surprise anyone who had come to think of it, when heard separately, as the ultimate cliché.

RUGGIERO LEONCAVALLO

Pagliacci

The Strolling Players

Opera in two acts (usually played as one), words and music by
Ruggiero Leoncavallo. The première took place at Teatro dal Verme,
Milan on May 21, 1892 with Adelina Stehle, Fiorello Giraud,
Victor Maurel, Mario Ancona and Francesco Daddi, conducted by
Arturo Toscanini.

CHARACTERS

Canio, *head of a troupe of strolling players*	Tenor
Nedda, *his wife*	Soprano
Tonio, *a clown*	Baritone
Beppe, *a clown*	Tenor
Silvio, *a villager*	Baritone

Villagers

Time: About 1865-70
Place: Montalto, in Calabria
Approx Length: 70 min.

Leoncavallo is said to have taken his story from a
real-life case tried by his father in his capacity as a
magistrate. The story is typical of the so-called
verismo school, with its lurid, slice-of-life tale and its
powerful and uninhibited musical style – more so, in
my view, than *Cavalleria*.

Act I.   In his prologue, Tonio asks the audience
to remember that the players are made of flesh and
blood like them. The action begins as the little
company arrives in a small village whose sole live
performance for the next few months they are that
evening to provide. Canio drums up trade for the
show, slaps down Tonio for his presumption and
over-reacts to a villager who wonders if he is to be
trusted with Nedda (aria: 'Un tal gioco', Such a
game). Bagpipers cause a diversion and Canio goes
off for a drink, leaving Nedda to dream of her young
lover (ballatella: 'Oh, che volo d'augelli', Oh, the
beautiful songbirds). Tonio makes up to her and is
seen off with a slash of the whip, but the arrival of
Silvio sparks off an extended love duet ('Decidi è il

mio destin', My destiny is decided/'E allor perchè,
di, tu m'hai stregato', Why then, tell me, have you
bewitched me). Tonio overhears and fetches Canio,
who fails to catch Silvio but demands that Nedda
reveal his name. She refuses and Beppe calms Canio,
who gets ready for the performance (aria: 'Vesti la
giubba', On with the motley).

Act II.   An intermezzo takes us to the evening's
performance. In the play-within-a-play, Harlequin
(Beppe) serenades Columbine (Nedda), before
Taddeo (Tonio) comes to make clumsy advances to
her. Harlequin sends him packing, but the advent of
Pagliaccio (Canio) causes a change of atmosphere
(aria: 'No, Pagliaccio non son', No, I am not
Pagliaccio) and the opera ends with the demented
Canio murdering first Nedda and then Silvio when
he comes to her aid.

Pagliacci caught the imagination even before its
first night, as can be seen by the cast of leading
singers Toscanini conducted. It contained in Stehle
and Maurel the Nannetta and Falstaff of the world

première of Verdi's *Falstaff* the following year; a Canio who a decade later was at la Scala to sing Siegfried with Toscanini; and in Ancona a Silvio whose records suggest a *bel canto* baritone to rival Battistini (Ancona was cast as Tonio for the opera's Metropolitan and Covent Garden premières).

Singers, like audiences, took immediately to the new opera. No baritone has a more grateful start to his evening than Tonio's prologue, with its histrionic banter with the audience, the music's rolling periods, the 'gift' top notes (one unwritten, like the top C in 'Di quella pira' in *Il trovatore*). If his opportunities thereafter somewhat decrease, the solo scene with Nedda provides him with a grand romantic tune of a kind more often given to tenors than to baritones.

Above left: *Nellie Melba and Fernando de Lucia, Covent Garden's first Nedda and Canio in 1893.*

Above right: *Enrico Caruso, whose Canio helped to establish the popularity of* Pagliacci.

Right: *Jon Vickers as Canio at the end of Zeffirelli's production at Covent Garden.*

The same could be said of Silvio's music, confined as it is to the extended love duet, in both sections of which he has so seductive a tune that the great Battistini was said regularly after the prologue to switch roles and expropriate Silvio for himself. So too did the tenor Richard Tauber, who in film and on

record sang at least the second part of the duet as if it had always been intended for tenor voice. Nedda comes to life in the ballatella, a challenging and rewarding solo whose brittle musical characteristics very effectively pin down her personality, shown in more passionate guise in the duet with Silvio.

The opera's great role is, of course, Canio, the clown whose breaking heart must not interfere with the evening's show. Few arias are better known out of context than his 'Vesti la giubba' though whether for the poignant situation, the passionate melody at the words 'Ridi, Pagliaccio' (Laugh, Pagliaccio) or for the sobs Caruso discreetly introduced just before the end it is hard to say. Canio is far from a one-aria role: his entrance music is discursive, but has some grand gestures ('A ventitre ore', Tonight at eleven); 'Un tal gioco' properly mixes melody with threat; and the role comes to a towering climax with 'No, Pagliaccio non son', a magnificent piece of breast-beating which wears its heart on its sleeve and brings the opera effectively to its melodramatic end – all guns firing and the audience pinned back into their seats with the vehemence, the sheer impact of it all. Perhaps this passage will serve if not as a definition, at least as a practical demonstration of what *verismo* means.

GIACOMO PUCCINI

La Bohème

The Bohemian Life

Opera in four acts by Giacomo Puccini; text by Giuseppe Giacosa and Luigi Illica, after Henri Murger's novel *Scènes de la vie de Bohème*. The première took place at Teatro Regio, Turin on February 1, 1896 with Elvira Cesira Ferrani, Pasini, Gorga, Wilmant, Mazzara and Pini-Corsi, conducted by Arturo Toscanini.

CHARACTERS

Rodolfo, *a poet*	Tenor
Marcello, *a painter*	Baritone
Colline, *a philosopher*	Bass
Schaunard, *a musician*	Baritone
Benoit, *a landlord*	Bass
Alcindoro, *a state councillor and Musetta's admirer*	Bass
Parpignol, *an itinerant toy vendor*	Tenor
Customs-house Sergeant	Bass
Musetta, *a grisette*[1]	Soprano
Mimi, *a seamstress*	Soprano

Students, Work Girls, Citizens, Shopkeepers, Street Vendors, Soldiers, Waiters, Boys, Girls, etc.

Time: About 1830
Place: Latin Quarter, Paris
Approx Act Lengths:
Act I 33 min., Act II 18 min., Act III 24 min., Act IV 18 min.

There is a story of Shostakovich asking Benjamin Britten what he thought of Puccini. 'He wrote terrible operas!', said Britten. 'No, Ben', said Shostakovich, 'he wrote marvellous operas, but terrible music'. A point of view I do not share, countless Puccini performances in the theatre having never left me approaching the next without a tingle of anticipation. To many opera-goers, in fact, Puccini is the quintessential Italian opera composer and *La Bohème* the quintessential opera. Here are the generous melody the words 'Italian opera' suggest, the warmth, the sheer memorability enjoyed and expected by hosts of people who listen to music.

Puccini had other qualities besides the gift of melody, crucial though that has been to his success. Foremost among them is a marvellous facility for the theatre, an ability to characterise and to turn every dramatic situation to his advantage. In *La Bohème* he shows additionally an epigrammatic quality which is new in his work (it was his fourth opera) and not seen again to the same degree until *Gianni Schicchi* twenty years later. As a kind of Italianate parallel to *Der Rosenkavalier*, in terms of putting across conversation concisely and with heightened

1. A Parisian girl, working often as a dress-maker or embroiderer. Always poorly paid, often of easy virtue.

Above: *Ricordi's poster for* La Bohème.

Above right: *The Café Momus in John Copley's production at Covent Garden.*

Below right: *The dying Mimi is brought back to the garret: Covent Garden, 1982.*

Above: *Rodolfo and Mimi meet in Act I of the original production.*

Below: *Mimi overhears Rodolfo and Marcello in Act III of the original production.*

expression, it is his masterpiece, but few of the listeners regularly bowled over by its melodic flow and memorability pause to notice that points are made (as the work's reputation does not bother to suggest) almost too fast for any but the connoisseur to take in.

La Bohème is a compilation of stories and characters taken from Henri Murger's picaresque novel, *Scènes de la vie de Bohème*, partly drawn from life, partly fictitious, involving the artists and grisettes among whom Murger lived.

Act I. Rodolfo and Marcello, to warm up the garret in which they live, burn the former's play. They are joined by Colline and Schaunard, who has earned some money and insists that they spend the evening at a café – after all, it is Christmas Eve. They bamboozle the landlord, Benoit, who has come for the rent, and leave Rodolfo to get on with an article. Mimi enters, saying her candle has gone out on the staircase, and, already half in love (aria for Rodolfo: 'Che gelida manina', How cold your little hand is. Aria for Mimi: 'Sì, mi chiamano Mimi', Yes, they call me Mimi), they go off together to the café (duet: 'O soave fanciulla', O lovely girl).

Act II. The street outside the Café Momus is full of people and Rodolfo introduces Mimi to his friends. Marcello's girl, Musetta, comes in with a rich admirer (aria: 'Quando m'en vo', When I am out walking), but contrives to get rid of him. The four friends and the two girls depart, leaving the bill to be presented to Musetta's admirer when he returns.

Act III. At a toll gate on the edge of Paris, officials quiz women bringing produce to market and Mimi tells Marcello that Rodolfo's jealousy is making life insupportable. Rodolfo emerges with the same kind of story (aria: 'Mimi è una civetta', Mimi is a minx), then admits that he thinks Mimi is very ill. Her coughing gives her hiding-place away and the act ends with a quartet, Mimi and Rodolfo turning their farewell into something like a reconciliation, but Musetta and Marcello quarrelling (quartet: 'Addio, dolce svegliare', Farewell, sweet awakenings).

Act IV. Back in the garret, Rodolfo and Marcello languish for departed love (duet: 'O Mimi, tu più non torni', Mimi, you'll return no more) and indulge in horseplay with their friends before

Jussi Björling as Rodolfo.

Musetta brings an exhausted Mimi upstairs. She is laid on the bed and the friends do what they can to help, but after a moment alone with Rodolfo, Mimi's strength gives out and she dies.

It has been argued that Puccini had a stronger feeling for theatre than for drama; that is to say, his *coups de théâtre* and his instinct for genre scenes are stronger than his ability to plan the grand picture. What is certain is that his musical eye for theatrical detail was extraordinary. In *La Bohème*, for instance, one has only to think of the musical planning of the tearing up of Rodolfo's manuscript to provide warmth; the manipulation of the key and the candles at Mimi's entrance; the combining of the soldiers' march with the Bohemians' retreat in Act II; Mimi's overhearing Rodolfo's conviction that she is mortally ill; the supremely well-contrasted quartet at the end of the same act; and the Bohemians' high spirits before the entry of the dying Mimi.

But in the end it boils down to melody. *La Bohème* is far from being a succession of arias; there are only six – two each for Rodolfo and Mimi in Acts I and

III, one for Musetta in Act II and a very short one for Colline in Act IV. All of them are well known, the four for the hero and heroine being among the most famous ever written. It is not only a question of arias: from the opening vocal phrases, there is a lilt to the score, its character coming from the combination of two essentially contrasting characteristics — a rhythmical brilliance associated with the extrovert features of the action (the Bohemians cavorting at home, the fun of the fair at Christmas) and the lyricism of the lovers.

All through, out of the rumbustious high spirits of the Bohemians or the hubbub of Christmas Eve will ascend tendrils of melody, mostly for the lovers (but by no means exclusively — Benoit is greeted by Marcello in the most expansive of phrases), but the score will still be remembered by the vast majority of listeners for the great outburst of warm lyricism which starts at the first sound of Mimi's voice, an outburst that continues to the end of the act; for that, and for Puccini's expression of the pathos of frustrated love.

Singers have liked the opera from its earliest days. It was Melba who took it to Covent Garden after its not very successful early English performances; and Melba again who took it to the Metropolitan in New York, arguing her way in each case against a reluctant management. But one must remember that it was not only the singers who appreciated the opera: Toscanini conducted the first performance and those two Melba premières had Mancinelli as conductor. None the less, all through history singers have loved to sing the music, from Caruso and Gigli to Björling and Pavarotti, from Melba and Muzio to de los Angeles and Freni. Like audiences, they know what makes them sound good.

GIACOMO PUCCINI

Tosca

Opera in three acts by Giacomo Puccini; text by Giuseppe Giacosa and Luigi Illica, after the play by Victorien Sardou. The première took place at Teatro Costanzi, Rome on January 14, 1900 with Hariclea Darclée, Emilio de Marchi and Eugenio Giraldoni, conducted by Leopoldo Mugnone.

CHARACTERS

Floria Tosca, *a celebrated singer*	Soprano
Mario Cavaradossi, *a painter*	Tenor
Baron Scarpia, *Chief of Police*	Baritone
Cesare Angelotti, *a political prisoner*	Bass
A Sacristan	Baritone
Spoletta, *a police agent*	Tenor
Sciarrone, *a gendarme*	Bass
A Gaoler	Bass
A Shepherd Boy (offstage)	Boy alto

Cardinal, Judge, Scribe, Officer, Sergeant, Soldiers, Police Agents, Ladies, Citizens, etc.

Time: June 1800
Place: Rome
Approx Act Lengths: Act I 44 min., Act II 42 min., Act III 28 min.

Though he had apparently known the play for some time, Puccini had a certain difficulty in securing *Tosca* as the subject for an opera. Another Italian composer, Alberto Franchetti, had already commissioned a libretto on the subject by the time Puccini settled on it and it took all the ingenuity (even, some may think, chicanery) at the command of Giulio Ricordi, who was Franchetti's publisher as well as Puccini's, to secure the subject for the composer whose work was likely to pay better dividends. Even before Puccini embarked on the new work, *Tosca*, like other plays by Sardou, was the object of a certain suspicion: its theatrical effectiveness tended to be written off as melodrama – what Shaw referred to as 'Sardoodledom'!

The opera was a success from the moment of its première, but a few months earlier the very experienced Ricordi had written scathingly to the

composer about the third act which he thought would 'cancel out the splendid impression of Act I . . . and the overwhelming effect Act II is bound to create'. He found the third act duet for Tosca and Cavaradossi 'fragmentary' and ends up by saying: 'Where in truth is the Puccini of that noble, warm and vigorous inspiration?'

All this may have been because Ricordi knew the third act to have been to some extent cobbled together from existing music waiting in Puccini's drawer to be put into an opera; and posterity might jib at the word 'noble', however much it approves the work as a whole. Certainly the American critic Joseph Kerman would reject it in view of his now well-known put-down of the opera as 'that shabby little shocker', a judgement which has probably won more notoriety for its author than it has done damage to *Tosca*. The general, public verdict would be much more favourable.

The events of the opera take place in 1800, when Italy was invaded by the French army. The Austrian General Melas is reported to have beaten Napoleon in battle and the consequent celebrations are likely to be attended by Queen Marie Caroline, wife of the Neapolitan King Ferdinand IV, daughter of Empress Maria Theresa and sister to Queen Marie Antoinette. Baron Scarpia is the much-feared Chief of Police.

Act I.   Angelotti, an escaped prisoner, takes refuge in the Church of Sant' Andrea della Valle, where Mario Cavaradossi, who shares Angelotti's republican sympathies, is painting a Mary Magdalene. Cavaradossi compares his blue-eyed Magdalene with the black-eyed Floria Tosca with whom he is in love (aria: 'Recondita armonia',

Antonio Scotti as Scarpia.

Strange harmony), recognises Angelotti and offers to help. Tosca's voice is heard outside. The ensuing love duet is coloured by her conviction that she heard a woman whispering inside (duet: 'Qual occhio al mondo', What eyes in the world). When she goes, Cavaradossi and Angelotti hurry away at the sound of the cannon shot denoting an escaped prisoner, and the returning Sacristan finds an empty church. Choir boys run riot at the prospect of extra pay for a *Te Deum* to celebrate Melas's victory, but Baron Scarpia erupts into their midst to question everyone and deduces that Angelotti may now be hiding at Cavaradossi's villa. When Tosca returns, Scarpia feeds her jealousy by showing her a fan he claims to have found on Cavaradossi's easel. Tosca departs, but Scarpia gives orders to have her followed, staying himself to join in the *Te Deum*.

Act II.   Scarpia in his apartment at the Farnese Palace plans a trap for Tosca, a prospect which arouses his lust. His sidekick, Spoletta, admits he found nothing at Cavaradossi's villa, but he did arrest the owner. Scarpia questions him. Tosca can be heard offstage singing a cantata and when she enters, Cavaradossi is taken off for interrogation. Tosca will answer no questions, but her nerve cracks when she realises her lover is under torture and she reveals Angelotti's hiding-place. Cavaradossi is brought in and rejoices at the news that Melas has in fact been defeated, before Tosca is manoeuvred into an infamous bargain (aria: 'Già mi dicon venal', They say that I am corrupt): Cavaradossi's life in exchange for her favours. Tosca prays (aria: 'Vissi d'arte', I have lived for art), but agrees to the deal. Scarpia gives Spoletta his orders: for form's sake there must be a public execution – simulated, 'just as in the case of Palmieri', he instructs Spoletta. Tosca alone does not know that Palmieri's execution was a 'mock' one using real bullets – the ultimate double-cross. Tosca and Scarpia are left together and as he gives her the safe conduct she needs, she stabs him to death.

Act III.   On the roof of Castel Sant' Angelo, Cavaradossi sings farewell to life (aria: 'E lucevan le stelle', The stars were shining). Tosca enters to be rapturously greeted by Cavaradossi and tells him that she has killed Scarpia with her own hands (aria: 'O dolci mani', O gentle hands). They sing of their life together in the future (duet: 'Amaro sol per te m'era il morire', Death for me was bitter only because of losing you) and Tosca coaches Cavaradossi in the art of playing dead. But the soldiers' bullets are real, Cavaradossi falls dead and, as she sees Spoletta who has discovered Scarpia's body, she leaps from the battlements.

Puccini's problem was, in a way, the same as faces all opera composers in a period when the avant garde is far ahead of public taste. Until the rise in the last quarter of the twentieth century of minimalists and of composers who take rock music as the basis for stage work, he might be said to have been the last

Right: *Ljuba Welitsch as Tosca, Vienna, 1950.*

Below: *Tito Gobbi and Maria Callas in Act II, Covent Garden, 1964.*

Above: *Franco Zeffirelli's detailed and effective set for Act I, Covent Garden, 1964.*

Left: *Ricordi's poster for the première of* Tosca, *Rome, 1900.*

'classical' composer apart from Gershwin to base his music on a demotic style, as Mozart had in *Die Zauberflöte*. His melodies are often not so far in cut from the *Piedigrotta*, Neapolitan song, the popular Italian idiom of the day, although Puccini himself was not Neapolitan and came from a distinguished family of Luccan composers. His tunes make more demands on the voice than those popular songs, so that it takes an opera singer to sing them; and their aspirations are higher, which is perhaps where Ricordi's word 'noble' comes in. Whatever they aspire to, Puccini's heroes and heroines are usually concerned with everyday emotions and activities – petty jealousies, likely love affairs, flirtations,

desertions, cheating at cards, favourite cities, wedding toasts, collections for indigent miners, and so on – and not, like Richard Strauss's, concerned with royal neurasthenia or the working out of Greek blood feuds, which makes the employment of a popular idiom as logical for Puccini as the use of the waltz for an Austrian.

In spite of 'Vissi d'arte' and Cavaradossi's three marvellous arias, *Tosca* is not an opera of solos – in fact, Puccini was reluctant to allow 'Vissi d'arte' to interrupt the drama of his second act, whose overwhelming effect Ricordi so confidently predicted. He has in many ways constructed his score to flow, often without intervention from the

Jonathan Miller's production, set in 1944 Rome (Malcolm Donnelly and Janice Cairns).

performers, like the incidental music to a film – sometimes introducing and always supporting dramatic events, regularly raising the temperature to involve the audience more fully, but mainly responding to the 'natural flow' of the drama. Puccini's inspiration works at such a high level that he has no need to strive for effect within that flow.

Cavaradossi is probably the most grateful of all Puccini's tenor roles, Tosca a candidate for the grandest and most rewarding of those for soprano. Like Manon, Mimi, Butterfly and Liu, she belongs in that category of threatened women whom Puccini loved to portray in music. Generations of prima donnas have revelled in the role's chances, from the Yugoslav Milka Ternina (who first sang it at Covent Garden and the Metropolitan), Emma Eames and Emmy Destinn early this century, through Jeritza (Puccini's declared favourite), Muzio, Lotte Lehmann and Cobelli, to the more recent Ljuba Welitsch, Zinka Milanov and Maria Callas. The music sits ideally on an Italianate *spinto* soprano's voice, the dramatic opportunities are varied and

spectacular and 'Vissi d'arte' is no more than the evening's crown – though it can be upstaged by the murder which follows and Tosca's elaborate ritual with the candles round Scarpia's body.

Scarpia is none the less probably the opera's biggest innovation – a villain who is sadist by confession and by his actions on stage, who gloats in persuasive music at the prospect of raping the heroine and is only prevented from doing it by his murder. It is a far cry from the villains of Donizetti or Bellini, even of Verdi. Perhaps Scarpia is the epitome of the *verismo* villain, as *Tosca's* second act is of *verismo* action. But even Scarpia has his solo moments. His entry is an arresting one (no pun is intended); the *Tè Deum* at the end of Act I is a most effective solo with chorus; Act II brings the monologue in which he exults in the prospect of forcible sex and the even more sinister passage in which he mocks Tosca's efforts to free herself from his trap. But, unless you apply the word to Scarpia's bargain, I do not think 'shabby' is the word which best describes it all.

GIACOMO PUCCINI

Madama Butterfly

Opera in three (originally two) acts by Giacomo Puccini; text by Giuseppe Giacosa and Luigi Illica, after the play by David Belasco. The première took place at la Scala, Milan on February 17, 1904 with Rosina Storchio, Giovanni Zenatello, and Giuseppe de Luca, conducted by Italo Campanini. It was a failure and there was only one performance, but in May 1904 at Brescia a revised version was successful with Salomea Krusceniski and Zenatello, conducted by Italo Campanini.

CHARACTERS

Cio-Cio-San (Madam Butterfly), *a geisha*	Soprano
Suzuki, *her maid*	Mezzo-soprano
Kate Pinkerton, *Pinkerton's wife*	Mezzo-soprano
Lieutenant B. F. Pinkerton, *of the US Navy*	Tenor
Sharpless, *American Consul at Nagasaki*	Baritone
Goro, *a marriage broker*	Tenor
Prince Yamadori, *a rich Japanese*	Baritone
The Bonze, *Cio-Cio-San's uncle*	Bass
The Imperial High Commissioner	Bass
The Official Registrar	Baritone
Trouble, *Cio-Cio-San's child*	Silent

Cio-Cio-San's Relations, Friends and Servants

Time: Early twentieth century
Place: Nagasaki
Approx Act Lengths: Act I 48 min., Act II 49 min., Act III 32 min.

Madama Butterfly, one of the world's most popular operas, provided at its première in Milan one of the great fiascos of operatic history. The public audibly objected to what it thought was a similarity between the theme of Butterfly's entrance (heard again at the climax of the love duet and also in Act II) and Mimi's first act aria in *La Bohème*, laughed at some of the action (which seems to have suffered from first night bad luck) and found the second act interminably long. The opera was withdrawn, but a revised version triumphed only three months later at Brescia; whether because of the changes Puccini had made, or because there was a heavier-voiced Butterfly (Krusceniski was famous for Brünnhilde and Salome), or because the public wanted to make amends to the composer, or simply because the performance was better than the one in Milan, it is hard to say. Cuts had been made; there was a new theme for entrance and love duet; Act II had been split up; and moreover, in the new Act III there was an aria for Pinkerton.

For 70 years history inaccurately held that this was the version which conquered audiences the world over, ignoring further changes made for Covent Garden in July 1905, for America in autumn 1906 and, at the request of the director, Albert Carré, for the Opéra-Comique in Paris in December 1906 (when Marguerite Carré was Butterfly,

Above: *The marriage ceremony in Sophie Fedorovich's supremely effective set at Covent Garden: this production, first seen in 1950, was regularly revived for over thirty years.*

Left: *Ricordi's poster for* Madama Butterfly.

Edmond Clément sang Pinkerton and Jean Périer, the original Pelléas, was Sharpless). For this 'final' version Puccini had cut from Act I the 'genre' scenes for Butterfly's relations (including an arietta for her inebriated uncle) and Pinkerton's ill-natured references to their habits. Revision elsewhere was also substantial, partly because the composer had second thoughts which were undoubtedly effective (consolidating, for example, the lullaby Butterfly sings as she carries the baby to bed), partly because he was persuaded – against his better judgement, some commentators think – that some of the libretto's first ideas were genuinely in advance of the audience's powers of acceptance (Sharpless's offer of money to Butterfly at Pinkerton's instigation, the portrayal of Mrs Pinkerton as a hard-edged intruder).

There is no doubt that the score Ricordi's published to coincide with the Paris performances embodied Puccini's final thoughts on the subject. The question is whether these were in fact his *best* thoughts; and current thinking tends to tease out a new version for every new production. In 1983, Paris mounted the *original* score, uncut and unimproved, and those of us who saw it felt the comment on *Madama Butterfly* we had witnessed was fascinating, but not one which should often be offered to a long-suffering public – and long *is* the

Mario Sammarco (Sharpless) and Giovanni Zenatello (Pinkerton) in an early performance.

Rosina Storchio, the original protagonist.

word, since the original added twenty minutes to normal running times.

Act I.   Pinkerton is shown his new house by Goro and greets Sharpless, who has come to oversee his 'wedding' to the geisha, Cio-Cio-San (duet: 'Amore o grillo', Is it love or fancy?). Her relations come with her, her uncle the Bonze denounces her decision to change her religion, but the act ends with an extended love duet.

Act II.   With Pinkerton gone, Butterfly has lived for three years with her son and Suzuki, believing he will eventually return (aria: 'Un bel dì

vedremo', One fine day we'll see). Sharpless calls to tell her Pinkerton is coming back with an American wife, but his visit is interrupted by the arrival of a suitor for Butterfly, Prince Yamadori, whom she rejects. None the less, when Sharpless gets his message through, her reaction is vigorous (aria: 'Che tua madre', That your mother) and by the end of the act she has watched Pinkerton's ship pass the harbour mouth and is, with her child and Suzuki, waiting for his arrival at the house.

Act III.   After an all-night vigil, Butterfly goes in to rest. Pinkerton arrives with Sharpless and is greeted by Suzuki (trio: 'Io so che alle sue pene', I know for such misfortunes), then leaves them to tell Butterfly the bad news (aria: 'Addio, fiorito asil, Farewell, house of flowers). Butterfly, confronted by Kate Pinkerton, says he may fetch his child in an hour's time, then commits suicide (aria: 'Tu, tu, piccolo iddio', You, you, my little god).

David Belasco's play, from which Puccini derived his opera, was only the latest in a series of Western reactions to the mystique of the Far East, most notably novels by Pierre Loti, the writings of Lafcadio Hearn and paintings by Whistler. Puccini not only introduced genuine Japanese music into his score, but also took pains to imitate Japanese musical style. The result is a mixture which imaginatively combines the exotic with his own brand of lyricism, sometimes on a small scale (like much of Act II), sometimes in his broadest manner (like the theme of Butterfly's entrance). There is nothing pedantically Japanese about his characterisation of Butterfly herself, who describes her knicknacks to Pinkerton in terms as Japanese as *sushi*, but whose contribution to the love duet matches the expansiveness of Pinkerton's own. The score is said to have been Puccini's favourite among his operas and Mosco Carner[1] calls it a 'psychological music-drama couched in the idiom of opéra-comique'. Could part of its initial lack of success have been due to a disparity of scale between the score and la Scala's auditorium? There are listeners who find sentimentality in the theme of the deserted geisha and her ineffably selfish lover, but rare is the musician who does not savour the score's loving detail and orchestral colouring as well as its great architectural span – Puccini's craft as well as his art.

The title role contains a challenge for any singer since it demands not only great vocal stamina and considerable power, but also some mastery of Japanese movement and gesture. The great protagonists have met these requirements, but it is interesting that the first Butterfly sang also Norina in *Don Pasquale* and Linda di Chamounix and returned to Butterfly for only a single performance some twenty years after the première, whereas the next

1. Mosco Carner: Puccini (Duckworth)

Geraldine Farrar as Butterfly, Metropolitan Opera, New York, 1907.

was a Brünnhilde; that Emmy Destinn, an Aida and a Senta, sang the role at Covent Garden; and that Toti dal Monte, a Lucia and a Gilda at la Scala, recorded the role in a prestigious pre-1940 set with Beniamino Gigli as Pinkerton – as wide, even disparate a range of vocal qualifications as any role could seek. The love duet would test a true *spinto*, but much of Act II is full of filigree detail well within the compass of a much lighter singer, although such a voice might later be taxed by 'Che tua madre' and the sheer length of the role.

Pinkerton is not exactly Puccini's most ambitious

Butterfly (Teresa Kubiak) kills herself: Covent Garden.

tenor part, though his music in Act I demonstrates an overt sexuality hard to find elsewhere in opera. The problem is that Act I requires a voice of real heft – without such endowment what is probably the composer's greatest love duet goes almost by default – and that the role peters out later, even though the much denigrated aria of the last act lets him go out, if not in glory, at least in some style.

Such has been *Butterfly*'s popularity over the years that the current fashion of re-working score and version seems almost like an indignity visited upon a public figure, distinguished but no longer young, but one must note that matters have not always stopped there. Re-examinations of the work there have been which keep scrupulously to the

spirit as well as the letter of the score – like Joachim Herz's in East Berlin and for Welsh National Opera; and there have been others which, it might be argued, have been less meticulous in maintaining Puccini's intentions, but have in the end been hardly less successful – like Ken Russell's production commissioned by the Spoleto Festival, in which the entire action takes place in a brothel of which Butterfly and Suzuki are both inmates and Butterfly goes through the 'mock' wedding specifically in order to improve her prospects. Only in the love duet did either detail or big picture start to ring false, which must speak loudly for what Belasco, Puccini, Giacosa and Illica left behind them and for the ultimate integrity of these updated views.

RICHARD STRAUSS

Der Rosenkavalier

The Knight of the Rose

Opera in three acts by Richard Strauss; text by Hugo von
Hofmannsthal. The première took place in Dresden on January 26,
1911 with Margarethe Siems, Minnie Nast, Eva von der Osten and
Karl Perron, conducted by Ernst von Schuch. The first performance in
Berlin was in April 1911 with Frieda Hempel, Claire Dux, Lola Artôt
de Padilla and Paul Knüpfer, conducted by Karl Muck.

CHARACTERS

Princess von Werdenberg, *the Feldmarschallin*	Soprano
Baron Ochs von Lerchenau	Baritone or Bass
Octavian, *brother of Count Rofrano*	Soprano
Baron von Faninal, *a wealthy parvenu*	Baritone
Sophie, *his daughter*	Soprano
Marianne, *her duenna*	Soprano
Valzacchi, *an Italian intriguer*	Tenor
Annina, *his partner*	Mezzo-soprano
A Police Commissary	Bass
Major domo to the Marschallin	Tenor
Faninal's major domo	Tenor
A notary	Bass
An Italian singer	Tenor
An Innkeeper	Tenor

Servants of the Marschallin, Four Waiters, A Little Black Page,
People attending the levée.

Time: The reign of Empress Maria Theresa
Place: Vienna
Approx Act Lengths: Act I 72 min., Act II 57 min., Act III 60 min.

Strauss had behind him two by no means negligible operas (*Guntram* and *Feuersnot*), and much of his most popular orchestral work, when at the age of forty he struck operatic gold. *Salome* (1905) and *Elektra* (1909) were his most innovative stage works, brilliant on their own account and influential in establishing Expressionism as a force on the German stage: he was not to blaze trails in quite this way again.

It was Hofmannsthal who, shortly after the première of their *Elektra*, suggested the subject of *Der Rosenkavalier* – a comedy set in Vienna in the time of Empress Maria Theresa and with two big roles, one for baritone and the other for a shapely girl in boy's clothes 'à la Farrar or Mary Garden' (as the writer suggested). No mention yet of the Marschallin, for many the most memorable of either Hofmannsthal's or Strauss's stage figures and often the dominating personality of a performance. Once again, the suggestion for collaboration had come from the Viennese sophisticate and was seized on with alacrity by the prolific (and more prosaic?)

Richard Mayr's classic portrayal of Ochs was first heard in Vienna in 1911.

Bavarian composer, who never thought of himself as on the intellectual level of his partner.

The opera was a success from the start, both in Dresden and in Berlin, though court etiquette in the German capital dictated some bowdlerisation of both stage directions and libretto. There was less emphasis on the bed and its occupants in the first scene and, in the libretto, on Ochs's keenness to chase anything in skirts. Ochs in Dresden was a baritone, Karl Perron, who had also been the first Jokanaan in *Salome* and the first Orestes in *Elektra*: one of the sadnesses of recording history is that he made no gramophone records. Indeed, a baritone able to tackle Wotan or Hans Sachs should find no problems in the score, but in Berlin a bass was cast. In Vienna later in 1911, the great bass Richard Mayr sang the role for the first of many times.

Like the singer of Baron Ochs, the original Marschallin, Margarethe Siems, was a regular at Strauss premières, but her list shows startling versatility. She was a Queen of the Night in *Die Zauberflöte* of some renown; in Dresden she sang Chrysothemis in *Elektra* and the Marschallin; and in Stuttgart she sang Zerbinetta in *Ariadne auf Naxos*. In Berlin, the three female leads were all exponents of the role of Violetta in *La traviata* (as is, in my view, ideal, Octavian requiring more a low soprano than a high mezzo) and in Dresden there had been two Violettas and an Isolde. Whatever the casting, the opera provides magnificent roles: it is not uncommon for a Sophie later to sing Octavian before graduating to the Marschallin, as did Lotte Lehmann and another great Strauss singer nearer our own day, Lisa della Casa.

Act I. In what is plainly a post-coital situation, the Marschallin assures her latest lover, the seventeen-year-old Octavian, that eventually he will look to someone nearer his own age and forget her. When voices are heard outside, Octavian disguises himself as a maid, emerging to find not the Marschallin's husband, but her country cousin, Baron Ochs, who has bullied his way in for an audience and immediately seems to fancy the young chambermaid. Ochs say he is to marry the heiress Sophie von Faninal and asks the Marschallin to choose for him a Knight of the Rose who will bear the customary symbol to his fiancée. She selects

Elisabeth Schumann (Sophie) receives the silver rose in Act II.

Octavian. At the Marschallin's levée, Ochs meets her attorney and two Italian intriguers, interrupts an Italian singer in full flight and leaves the Marschallin to brood on the tragedy of growing old. No comforting words from Octavian on his return can relieve her melancholy.

Act II. In his salon the *nouveau riche* Baron von Faninal, his daughter Sophie and her duenna wait for the ceremonial arrival of the Rosenkavalier. Ochs follows him in and so disgusts Sophie with his coarse manners that, when he leaves with Faninal, she and Octavian fall into each other's arms. The Italian

HUGO·VON·HOFMANNSTHAL~RICHARD·STRAUSS?·OPERA·BUFFA·

BÜHNENBILD·FÜR·DEN·2·AUFZUG·EIN·SAAL·IM·PALAIS·HERRN·VON·FANINALS

Above: *Alfred Roller's design for Octavian's entry in Act II. Only the over-exuberant stoves suggest this is the house of the 'nouveau riche' Baron von Faninal.*

Right: *Kiri Te Kanawa as the Marschallin in Act I at Covent Garden.*

couple summon Ochs and Octavian demands satisfaction in a duel. Ochs is lightly pinked, but easily comforted with a glass of wine. He ends the act humming his favourite waltz and, with the aid of one of the Italian go-betweens, arranging (as he thinks) an assignation with the Marschallin's chambermaid.

Act III. The intrigue hots up as Octavian, disguised as the maid Mariandel, rehearses Valzacchi and his accomplices in the tricks they will later play on Ochs. The rendezvous goes more or less to plan, but Ochs is sufficiently put out to summon help: the arrival of the police poses more problems than it solves. Ochs's servants in their panic have also called for help from Faninal and the Marschallin: when the latter makes her entry, the dénouement is at hand. She dismisses Ochs (who belatedly sees through the Octavian-Mariandel imbroglio), consoles Sophie and, in a gesture of renunciation, leaves the young lovers alone together – as she has always promised herself she would.

Der Rosenkavalier has probably been performed more often than any other German opera written in the twentieth century. In its own way, it is a masterpiece – also, a parade of paradox and pastiche. For the orchestra (112 instruments, including 19 on the stage in Act III) the music is as complicated and hard to play as anything of the dodecaphonic school, yet it must sound as mellifluous and effortless as Mozart. All is contrivance, an evocation of an unrealistic, fairytale Vienna of long ago, when everyone was witty, everything was elegant, the action was a little *risqué* and all could be forgiven provided it was done with

style. So attractive is the creation that the city's inhabitants have come to believe in its reality and even, I have been told, point out *Rosenkavalier* landmarks as if they had once existed.

The principal means Strauss and Hofmannsthal employ are either anachronistic, like the ubiquitous and magical waltzes, which perfectly suggest a period atmosphere of which they were never part; or else pure invention, like the plausible but unhistorical presentation of a rose to an engaged girl. That never happened, but it *seems* as if it could have done. It suggested to Strauss one of his most magical and grandest set pieces, with a glistening, ice-cold orchestral texture (oboe against chords on flutes, harps, solo violins and celesta) to underpin Sophie's soaring vocal rapture, which is in itself one

Left: *Josephine Barstow (the Marschallin) and Sally Burgess (Octavian), English National Opera.*

Below: *Richard Van Allan (Ochs) and Lois McDonall (the Marschallin), English National Opera.*

of the major exemplars of the composer's idiomatic way of writing for the soprano voice.

In a way, in all his operas Strauss longed for the set piece which opera early on established as a main means of expression – in *Salome*, think of the orchestra as Jokanaan leaves and returns to the cistern, of the dance, of Salome's peroration; or in *Elektra*, of the recognition scene and Elektra's triumphant dance (the latter, I think, not a total success). So in *Rosenkavalier* we have both the presentation of the rose early in Act II and the waltz at the end; the opera's extraordinary prelude, with its themes brilliantly evocative of male and female characteristics and in combination depicting love-making as nowhere else in music; the folk-like duet for Sophie and Octavian just before the opera's end; and above all the great trio for the three soprano voices. This trio perhaps contains the greatest paradox of all. The Marschallin's renunciation of Octavian, his gratitude and Sophie's ecstatic reaction lead to an ensemble of great beauty and both musically and dramatically to a point of catharsis – but Strauss has built the great edifice on an extended version of a trumpery (if memorable) ditty earlier associated with Octavian in drag as Mariandel! Great things truly have small beginnings!

The mind could be forgiven for boggling – just as it might at the idea of all those Viennese waltzes written out of period by a Bavarian – were it not for the musicality of the whole achievement. One of the fine fruits of the collaboration is a new kind of musical conversation, which is sometimes slow and lyrical, as in the scene for the Marschallin and Octavian at the start of Act I, and sometimes fast-moving, as with Ochs, the Marschallin and Octavian – a unique example of speech heightened by music which neither descends to banality nor blurs the conversational outline. On this basis, Strauss was able to construct passages of genuine pathos, such as the Marschallin's reflections on the passing of youth and the foreseen need eventually to renounce Octavian.

LEOŠ JANÁČEK

Její Pastorkyňa (Jenůfa)

Her Stepdaughter

Opera in three acts by Leoš Janáček; text by the composer, after a play by Gabriella Preissová. The première took place in Brno on January 21, 1904 with Marie Kabeláčová, Leopolda Svobodová, Steněk-Doubravaský and Procházka.

CHARACTERS

Grandmother Buryjovka, *owner of the mill*	Contralto
Half-brothers	
Laca Klemeň	Tenor
Števa Buryja	Tenor
Kostelnička Buryjovka	Soprano
Jenůfa, *her stepdaughter*	Soprano
Foreman at the Mill	Baritone
Mayor of the village	Bass
His wife	Mezzo-soprano
Karolka, *his daughter*	Mezzo-soprano
A maid	Mezzo-soprano
Barena, *servant at the mill*	Soprano
Jano, *shepherd boy*	Soprano
An old woman	Contralto

Musicians, Village People

Time: Nineteenth century
Place: A village in Moravia
Approx Act Lengths: Act I 45 min., Act II 53 min., Act III 31 min.

Jenůfa, written over a period of ten years, was its composer's first great success (at the age of fifty), the first work by which he became a celebrity outside Brno, not only in the Czech capital, Prague, but in Vienna and the world at large. By ill luck, the head of the Prague Opera, Karel Kovařovic, bore Janáček a grudge because of a bad press notice some years before and only after extraordinary efforts by the composer's admirers would he accept *Jenůfa* for Prague. Even then he stipulated that he should 'edit' the work and for years the opera was heard only in his version (some re-orchestration and a large number of tiny cuts), a disfigurement which performing practice, led by Charles Mackerras, has started to put right.

For his operas, Janáček drew on two sources: folk music, which he tended to compose in imitation rather than quote; and the speech rhythms and inflections of the Moravians among whom he lived. He kept notebooks in which he notated what he had heard in the market-place, in the street, at the dinner-tables of friends. As a result, his operas are full of ejaculatory phrases which punctuate the lyricism he could just as convincingly employ, and

Ashley Putnam as Jenůfa at Covent Garden in 1986.

part of the music's character comes from these contrasting ingredients.

Long before *Jenůfa* begins, Grandmother Buryjovka has had two sons, each of them now dead. The elder, who inherited the family mill, married the Widow Klemeň, who already had a son, Laca. Together, she and the miller had another son, Števa. Grandmother Buryjovka's second son, Tomas Buryja, had by his first wife a daughter named Jenůfa. After the death of Jenůfa's mother, Tomas Buryja married the woman we know only as Kostelnička, because as a widow she became Sacristan to the village chapel. Števa and Jenůfa are therefore first cousins, Laca no blood relation to the Buryja family.

Originally, Janáček composed a full-scale overture for Jenůfa, but it was not used in Brno in 1904 nor in 1916 in Prague, though it has had fairly frequent concert performances under the title *Zarlivost* – Jealousy.

Act I.   The scene is a mill in the mountains in late afternoon. The prelude has running through it the tinkling sound of the mill wheel – created by a xylophone – and this recurs throughout the opera.

Laca (Kolbjörn Höiseth) slashes Jenůfa's face (Elisabeth Söderström) in Götz Friedrich's splendid Stockholm production (1972).

Old Grandmother Buryjovka peels potatoes, Laca with his knife is shaping a whip-handle and Jenůfa, standing nearby, begins to wonder despairingly whether Števa, whom she loves and by whom (unknown to the others) she is pregnant, has been recruited for the army.

Laca is odd man out at the mill and he makes sarcastic reference to his conviction that he is only worth his food and lodging because of the work he can do: Števa is Grandmother Buryjovka's pet! In the orchestra, Janáček shows compassion for the foibles and misfortunes of his characters, but Laca in song and action seems uncompromisingly bitter, so much so that Jenůfa takes him to task for the way in which he talks to her grandmother. Jano, the shepherd boy, brings a note of exuberance into the music as he sings out that he can now really read.

The work of the mill continues and the foreman offers to sharpen Laca's knife. Jenůfa and Laca continue their verbal sparring, until the foreman reacts vigorously to Laca's outward cynicism and warns him about his attitude towards Jenůfa. Anyhow, he has heard that Števa has not been taken for a soldier, news which Jenůfa and Grandmother Buryjovka greet with delight. Kostelnička appears and goes into the mill, and Grandmother Buryjovka suggests they follow her, but Jenůfa stays behind to welcome Števa back.

Young men are heard singing jauntily and they are egged on by Števa, who is so drunk he can hardly walk. Jenůfa is almost hysterical with delight to see him and tries to bring him to his senses while he instructs his companions to sing and dance for the entertainment of him and his Jenůfa. All seems quite festive on the surface, until Kostelnička brings it to a sudden stop and reads the company a lecture mainly aimed at her rich nephew, Števa. There can be no more talk of a wedding with Jenůfa until he proves that he has stopped drinking by a year of sobriety.

Grandmother Buryjovka rather ineffectually tries to put a good face on it, sends the musicians packing and tells Števa to go and sleep it off. The scene ends with a short *fugato* in which Grandmother Buryjovka warns Jenůfa that life is full of sorrow. Foreman, Laca, chorus and finally Jenůfa herself follow her lead, as the xylophone suggests that the life of the mill goes on in the background.

Alone with Števa, Jenůfa pleads her love and her fear that her secret may be discovered. Her plea becomes a confession, dragged out of her in short ejaculatory phrases, and its tenderness is hard to resist. Števa's still fuddled reaction is little more than conventional gallantry and for a moment Jenůfa loses control. Laca returns to find her sunk in misery and, trying to provoke her into some hostility towards Števa's selfish behaviour, says that Števa only loves her for her rosy-apple cheeks. She continues to defend him. Laca seems about to embrace her, but instead slashes her across the cheek with his knife.

She runs into the house screaming, while Laca laments the horrible thing he has done. It was all an accident, suggests Barena, but the foreman takes Laca aside and accuses him, for all his present remorse, of having committed the crime on purpose.

Act II. The living-room of Kostelnička's house five months later. The music shows an atmosphere tense from the start, as Kostelnička and Jenůfa sit sewing, the latter's wound still livid on her cheek. The baby was born, but it is weeks since Jenůfa last saw his father. Jenůfa goes inside, leaving the baby sleeping peacefully. Everything she says reveals her joy in the child, every utterance of Kostelnička her shame and misery. Kostelnička gives Jenůfa a drink with a narcotic to make her sleep and Jenůfa goes into the bedroom.

Kostelnička admits to herself that she has prayed the child might die, but now is resigned to the notion of Jenůfa and Števa marrying. Števa comes to visit and she scolds him for not having been before. He seems not to want to see Jenůfa and his son and makes clear his resentment that her beauty has been spoilt: this means the end of his love for her. Of course the child will have money − but no-one must know that it is his.

This is what Kostelnička feared and, as Števa says, her pleas would melt the heart of a stone. They grow in intensity, but Števa eventually blurts out that he is engaged to marry the Mayor's daughter, Karolka. He runs out and, as Kostelnička screams in horror, Jenůfa's voice can be heard calling in her sleep from the next room. Kostelnička is left alone brooding on the problem which it seems she must attempt to solve entirely on her own.

When Laca comes in, Kostelnička cannot find it in her to dissemble any longer and tells him about the child. Laca instinctively reacts against the idea: marrying Jenůfa, which he dearly wants to do, involves taking Števa's baby! Kostelnička sees Jenůfa's last chance slipping away from her and tells him that the baby died. She is left alone to face the facts as they are and the facts as she has presented them. She wrestles with her conscience and we hear agony and indecision in the music as she decides there is no other way but to kill the baby. She rushes out with him into the night.

Jenůfa, still half-drugged, wakes up and calls for Kostelnička. She looks at the stars and suddenly

Jenůfa (Elisabeth Söderström) comforts Kostelnička (Kjerstin Meyer) in Act III of the Stockholm production.

realises her baby is not there. She is all agitation, but decides Kostelnička must have taken him to show to Števa. She prays for his future and the music's sadness and tenderness are dispelled for a moment when Kostelnička comes back in a state of utmost agitation. It returns after Jenůfa hears that her child has died, Kostelnička explaining that Jenůfa has been unconscious and delirious for two days and that in that time the baby died and was buried. Jenůfa must forget Števa, says Kostelnička, and when Laca returns, his joy at seeing Jenůfa again is touching in its sincerity. Jenůfa is at first dignified and distant, but Laca's tenderness overcomes her reserve. Kostelnička starts to think that her action has been justified and has put everything right, but she is wrong: windows blow open and the wind brings with it a sense of doom and disaster. Kostelnička howls in terror: 'It's as if death were peering into the house!'

Act III.   In Kostelnička's house Jenůfa and Laca sit waiting for the wedding guests to arrive. Kostelnička is in a state of nervous exhaustion and the appearance of the Mayor to offer congratulations causes even more agitation. Karolka and Števa come to congratulate the happy couple, but Karolka plays up when Števa says they are to be married in two weeks' time and says she may yet change her mind. Barena leads a group of girls in singing a wedding song and Grandmother Buryjovka blesses the happy couple.

Suddenly, there are cries outside. A baby's body has been found in the mill-stream and the Mayor and guests hurry out. Kostelnička becomes hysterical, but the voice of Jenůfa can be heard crying that the baby is hers. Feeling against her rises until the mob seems ready to stone her for what they think must be her crime. They fall silent when Kostelnička tells them that the guilt is hers and hers alone. Jenůfa has a moment of revulsion, but it is only too clear that Kostelnička committed her crime in an effort to do good; and Jenůfa's great effort of forgiveness somehow redeems what Kostelnička has done. Kostelnička seems about to commit suicide, but remembers she must stand as a witness

if Jenůfa is not to suffer for something of which she is wholly guiltless.

Jenůfa and Laca are left together. Jenůfa feels her life must now be lived out alone, but Laca begs to be allowed to share it. His reward is Jenůfa's great cry of joy as she comes finally – the music tells us this – to love him. Their duet, added to the score after the première and given a different orchestral accompaniment by Kovařovic, has a freshness of its own and the quality of Laca's devotion is pointed up by situation and music alike.

Following *Jenůfa*, over the next thirteen years Janáček wrote two operas – *Osud* (Fate), an unconventional piece in cinematic, conversational style, and a fantastic burlesque, *The Adventures of Mr Brouček*. The former was not staged in his lifetime and the latter only gradually accepted after his death. After this period of relative obscurity, the final flowering of his genius was generated by his meeting with a young married woman, Kamila Stösslová, with whom he fell in love in 1917: his musical fecundity between the ages of 63 and 74 was limitless. *Katya Kabanova* (1921), *The Cunning Little Vixen* (1924), *The Makropoulos Affair* (1926) and the posthumous *From The House of The Dead* were accompanied by works in all musical forms conventional and unconventional: there can hardly have been within a ten-year span a more diverse *oeuvre* in all operatic history.

GEORGE GERSHWIN

Porgy and Bess

Opera in three acts by George Gershwin; text by Du Bose Heyward
and Ira Gershwin. The première took place in Boston on September
30, 1935 with Todd Duncan as Porgy, Anne Brown as Bess, Warren
Coleman as Crown, Eddie Matthews as Jake and Bubbles as Sportin'
Life, conducted by Alexander Smallens.

CHARACTERS

Porgy, *a cripple*	Bass-baritone
Bess, *Crown's girl*	Soprano
Crown, *a tough stevedore*	Baritone
Serena, *Robbins's wife*	Soprano
Clara, *Jake's wife*	Soprano
Maria, *keeper of the cook-shop*	Contralto
Jake, *a fisherman*	Baritone
Sportin' Life, *a dope pedlar*	Tenor
Mingo	Tenor
Robbins, *an inhabitant of Catfish Row*	Tenor
Peter, *the honeyman*	Tenor
Frazier, *a black 'lawyer'*	Baritone
Annie	Mezzo-Soprano
Lily, *Peter's wife, strawberry woman*	Mezzo-soprano
Jim, *a cotton picker*	Baritone
Undertaker	Baritone
Nelson	Tenor
Crab man	Tenor

Speaking Parts
Mr Archdale, *a white man*
Detective
Policeman
Coroner
Scipio, *a small boy*

Time: 'Recent past'
Place: Catfish Row, Charleston, South Carolina, USA
Approx Act Lengths: Act I 60 min., Act II 53 min., Act III 85 min.

Gershwin was not the only figure with his roots in
jazz and American show business to attempt opera
as a form: the great Scott Joplin, twenty years before
Porgy and Bess saw the stage, had saddled himself
with a wishy-washy, Uncle-Tom's-Cabin libretto for
his *Treemonisha*, which none the less contains much
attractive music. Gershwin himself seems to have
been a little diffident in face of the new medium and
in spite of the unquestioned, even triumphant
success of the score as a whole, he not only found a

Leontyne Price and William Warfield as Porgy and Bess, 1952.

certain difficulty in using accompanied recitative, but, in search presumably of incident and variety, risked burdening the score with a quantity of 'character' numbers, which make agreeable musical points but do little for the drama. Not all these episodes figured in the production the composer himself supervised and their restoration may be found to confirm his theatrical instincts. None the less, an outstanding opera it is, the first from America to make a substantial world-wide success and the only opera based on the jazz of the 1920s and 1930s to survive the war which effectively put an end to the period.

Act I. The first scene is set in the courtyard of the tenement. The first half establishes the variegated night-life of Catfish Row – we get a piano playing a 'low-down' blues, singing and dancing, Clara singing a lullaby to her baby, a crap game gradually taking over. Jake, Clara's husband, offers to help sing the baby to sleep. What differentiates this from other operas is that Clara's lullaby is 'Summertime', whose lyrical beauty makes it one of the best-known songs of our century, and that Jake's 'A woman is a sometime thing' is only a little less memorable.

Peter, the honeyman, is heard calling his wares before the crippled Porgy comes into the courtyard. Everyone likes Porgy – Jake gives his opinion that 'he's soft on Crown's Bess' – and Porgy sticks up for Bess when the others attack her. Crown and Bess make their entrance, Crown drunk and morose but keen to join the crap school. When he turns out to be too unsteady to read the dice, the others laugh at him and his temper boils over. He throws Robbins to the ground and kills him with a cotton hook. Bess slips him some money and he sobers up enough to say that any arrangement she may make while he is in hiding is strictly temporary: he will be back. Sportin' Life – throughout the opera a man with an eye to the main chance – suggests to Bess that they go to New York together, but she spurns the offer and tries to get someone – anyone – to take her in. Porgy opens his door to her just as the first police whistles are heard.

The second scene is in Serena's room, where there is mourning. Robbins body is laid out on the bed with a saucer on its chest to collect money for the burial. Porgy and Bess contribute and mourners exhort each other to follow their example. Porgy joins a rhythmic spiritual before a detective puts his head round the door and accuses Peter of the murder. The others say that Crown did it, but the detective arrests the protesting and inoffensive Peter as a 'material witness'. Porgy derides the inadequacy of a justice which hauls off a harmless old man and leaves a criminal like Crown wandering about scot-free. The wake continues and Serena begins a grandiose lament, 'My man's gone now', in which the chorus supports her. In the end the undertaker agrees to bury Robbins for the $15 in the saucer and Bess leads the last of the Spirituals, 'Oh, we're leavin' for the Promise' land', which ends the act on a note of anticipation.

Act II. It is a month later. Jake and other fishermen get ready to go to sea: 'It take a long pull

Willard White as Porgy at Glyndebourne, 1986.

The Crap Game at Glyndebourne: the opera was designed by John Gunter and Sue Blane and produced by Trevor Nunn.

to get there'. The forecast is for storms, but there is a mood of optimism all round as Porgy sings his Banjo song, 'I got plenty o' nuttin',' a brilliant piece with an infectious lilt. Everyone comments on the change in him since Bess came to live with him.

The life of Catfish Row is always on the go and in succession we see Maria giving Sportin' Life a piece of her mind for peddling dope; Lawyer Frazier selling Porgy a divorce for Bess (harder – and dearer – for someone not even married, he explains); and Mr Archdale paying a visit to tell Porgy he will go bail for the jailed Peter. Porgy in his Buzzard Song, which is sometimes omitted, explains that the bird is ill-omened and if it alights on a building it will bring bad luck to everyone there. Sportin' Life smells pickings and sneaks up to Bess, suggesting they team up; but Bess is adamant she has finished once and for all with the 'happy dust'. Porgy realises what is going on and grabs Sportin' Life's wrist in a grip of iron, warning him to keep his hands off Bess.

It is the day of the organised picnic and everybody goes off to get ready, leaving Porgy alone with Bess. Their love duet, 'Bess, you is my woman now', is one of the great numbers of the score (it was even sung at the centenary celebrations of the Statue of Liberty) and at its end a military band strikes up and the picnickers are on their way.

The scene changes to Kittiwah Island in the evening of the same day. After dancing and a general shindig on the part of the picnickers, Sportin' Life treats them to a sermon in praise of the virtues of scepticism, whose jaunty tune and brilliant lyrics have made it one of the score's most popular numbers: 'It ain't necessarily so'. Serena scolds them as a pack of sinners, incidentally reminding them that they must hurry on board before the boat leaves. Bess lags behind and finds Crown standing in front of her. He will be back for her in a couple of weeks, he says, but she pleads to be allowed to stay with Porgy, who has taught her to live decently. Crown laughs: her life with Porgy is temporary. He should find another woman, she sings ('Oh, what you want wid Bess?'), but in the end she finds Crown irresistible and is left behind when the boat leaves.

The third scene of the act is set back in Catfish Row some days later. Jake is preparing to go off fishing, Peter has returned from jail and Bess's voice comes from Porgy's room. She disappeared for two whole days and is still delirious. Serena prays for her to get well. The attractive cries of strawberry woman, honeyman and crab man are registered, after which the voice of Bess is heard, evidently on the road to recovery. Porgy knows she has been with Crown, but says it makes no difference. 'I loves you, Porgy', she sings, and Porgy promises to take care of Crown if he returns. Meanwhile, Clara has been anxiously watching the sea and the sound of the hurricane bell brings the scene to an end.

For the fourth scene we are back in Serena's room. The storm rages outside and inside all pray. Kittiwah Island must be under water, they say, but someone bangs at the door and Crown staggers in calling for Bess. He throws Porgy down when he intervenes and stops the keening with a cheerful jazzy number: 'A red-headed woman makes a chow-chow jump its track'. Suddenly, Clara sees Jake's boat floating upside down in the river and rushes out. Bess urges some man to follow her, but the only one tough enough is Crown, whose parting word is to promise to come back for Bess.

Act III.   In the courtyard there is general sorrow for Clara, Jake and Crown, all of whom they suppose lost in the storm. Sportin' Life mocks the notion of mourning for Crown and wonders what will happen when there is a confrontation over Bess. Meantime, Bess sings 'Summertime' as she looks after Clara's baby (the only time she gets to sing what is effectively Clara's number) and the court gradually empties. Suddenly, Crown can be seen at the gate. As he passes Porgy's window, an arm is silently extended to plunge a knife into his back. He staggers upright and is seized round the neck in Porgy's iron

Porgy (Willard White) catches Sportin' Life (Damon Evans) with Bess (Cynthia Haymon): Glyndebourne, 1986.

The arrival of Porgy (Willard White): Glyndebourne, 1986.

grip and slowly throttled. 'Bess, you got a man now, you got Porgy.'

The next scene takes place the next afternoon. The police question Serena, who says she has been ill and knows nothing about the death of Crown, even though everyone knows he killed her husband. Porgy is roped in to identify Crown, but will not look at the body, his reluctance fed by Sportin' Life's helpful dictum that Crown's wounds will bleed when the murderer comes into the body's presence. He is taken off to jail and Sportin' Life offers Bess some 'happy dust' to tide over her nerves, which she tries unsuccessfully to refuse. Sportin' Life sings a persuasive Blues, 'There's a boat dat's leavin' soon

for New York', and leaves a second packet of dope. Bess sneaks out to pick it up.

It is a week later, morning in Catfish Row and everything back to normal. Children are dancing and Porgy has returned from a week in jail for contempt of court. He distributes presents but knows something is wrong when he sees Serena holding Clara's baby. 'Oh Bess, oh, where's my Bess?' he sings and Serena and Maria join in, the one excusing and the other condemning Bess for going off with Sportin' Life. Porgy ends the opera on a note of hope as he sings 'Oh, Lord, I'm on my way', and starts off in his goat-cart to find Bess wherever she may have gone and bring her home.

BENJAMIN BRITTEN

Peter Grimes

Opera in a prologue, three acts and an epilogue by Benjamin Britten; text by Montagu Slater, after the poem, *The Borough*, by George Crabbe. In America in 1941 Britten read an article by E. M. Forster on the subject of Crabbe, a poet from East Anglia. Soon afterwards, Serge Koussevitsky, the conductor, offered to commission him to write an opera and in the spring of 1942, after he had returned to England, he and Montagu Slater started work on the libretto. The story is a free adaptation of Crabbe, but the venue remains Aldeburgh, Crabbe's birthplace, where Britten subsequently made his home. The première was in London on June 7, 1945 at Sadler's Wells, which boldly reopened with the new opera after wartime closure. Peter Pears sang the title role, with Joan Cross, Edith Coates, Valetta Iacopi, Roderick Jones, Edmund Donlevy, Owen Brannigan, Morgan Jones and Tom Culbert, conducted by Reginald Goodall. The opera's instant success seemed at the time to open a new, and for the time being, confident chapter in British music.

CHARACTERS

Peter Grimes, *a fisherman*	Tenor
John, *his apprentice*	Silent
Ellen Orford, *a widow, schoolmistress*	Soprano
Captain Balstrode, *retired merchant skipper*	Baritone
Auntie, *landlady of 'The Boar'*	Contralto
Her two 'Nieces', *main attractions of 'The Boar'*	Soprano
Bob Boles, *Methodist fisherman*	Tenor
Swallow, *a lawyer*	Bass
Mrs Sedley, *widow*	Mezzo-soprano
Rev. Horace Adams, *the rector*	Tenor
Ned Keene, *apothecary and quack*	Baritone
Dr. Crabbe	Silent
Hobson, *the carrier*	Bass

Townspeople and Fisherfolk

Time: Towards 1830
Place: The Borough, a fishing village on the East coast of England
Approx Act Lengths: Act I 55 min., Act II 52 min., Act III 42 min.

Peter Grimes has probably had more performances than any other full-scale opera written since 1945: its nearest rival might be Stravinsky's *The Rake's Progress*. The music's vitality and invention go with a treatment large enough in scale to appeal to older opera-goers, while the personality of Grimes, the anti-hero, has made the work sufficiently different to attract the more sophisticated younger listeners.

Prologue. In the Borough's Moot Hall, an

inquest (in a kind of heightened recitative) is being held on Grimes's apprentice. The populace feels Grimes's brutality has caused the boy's death, but his evidence suggests that his boat was driven off course while he was out fishing and, after three days without water, the boy died of exposure. The more lively citizens of the Borough confirm the evidence, some sympathetic to Grimes, some hostile, and the Coroner gives his verdict: '. . . your apprentice died in accidental circumstances. But that's the kind of thing people are apt to remember.' After Grimes's vain attempts to make himself heard, the court is cleared. Ellen Orford tries to comfort him, their unaccompanied duet starting in different keys and gradually coming together ('Your voice out of the pain . . .').

Act I.   An orchestral passage joins prologue and act, the first of the so-called Interludes: each act begins with one and has one in the middle, and the pieces together form a concert suite. The passage establishes the movement of waves and water which begins each new day for the fishermen. The scene is basically choral (mending nets and sails, baiting lines), but its even tenor is frequently interrupted in

Peter Pears, the first Peter Grimes, at Sadler's Wells, 1945.

vivid musical terms – by Bob Boles, who objects to anything likely to be fun; by Balstrode, who frets about the weather; by the morning greeting of the Rector, Mrs Sedley and Mr Swallow; by Ned Keene, who wants an assignation that night with one of Auntie's 'Nieces'; and finally by Grimes, who calls for help with his boat. It is forthcoming only from Balstrode and Keene, the latter saying that he has found Grimes another apprentice who must be fetched from the workhouse. Carter Hobson at first (in what Britten calls a 'half number') will have nothing to do with it, but Ellen Orford offers help. When the villagers object – a first hint of mob feeling – Ellen stands firm: 'Let her among you without fault cast the first stone.' Hobson agrees to do the job.

Balstrode sees through his binoculars that the storm cone has been hoisted and leads a massive fugal ensemble which ends with a prayer and in its course establishes the storm music which is to dominate the rest of the act. Balstrode stays to comment on Grimes's apparently determined stand as a 'loner' and to suggest that he should work on a merchantman, out of reach of the Borough's gossip. Grimes protests: 'I am native, rooted here/By familiar fields, marsh and sand.' He is still haunted by the horrifying experience alone at sea with the corpse of his apprentice, but plans to stop gossip with the one thing people listen to – money. The duet grows in intensity as he first rejects Balstrode's advice and then reflects passionately on the peace which could be his if Ellen were to be his wife. The interval of the ninth seems to illustrate Grimes's maladjustment and in its minor form infects the early part of the scene with Balstrode, resolving into the major as Grimes dreams of Ellen and a new life.

The interlude which introduces the second scene of the act is concerned with the storm (apart from a reference to Grimes's longing for something better) and even when the curtain rises to show the interior of The Boar Inn, the storm remains as background, taking over orchestrally each time one of the characters opens the door and lets in wind and rain. Until Grimes's entrance the music is episodic, first of all revealing Mrs Sedley as an infrequent visitor, waiting for Ned Keene; then dominated by Auntie pithily answering Balstrode's complaint about the

The Borough works itself up to hunt Grimes down (Covent Garden).

noise the frightened 'Nieces' are making; later observing Bob Boles's drunken and obstreperous advances to one of them, until he is calmed by Balstrode who leads the company in 'We live and let live, and look we keep our hands to ourselves'. Grimes enters and seems not to notice that he has an adverse effect on the atmosphere but sings introspectively of the mystery of the skies and of human destiny: 'Now the Great Bear and Pleiades'. The orchestra has the melody, but, even though it has a contrasting *molto animato* passage in the middle, the *scena* has been described as a one-note aria, culminating in the suggestive and reiterated: 'Who, who, who, who can turn skies back and begin again?', which makes this one of the opera's most haunting moments.

The crowd, particularly Bob Boles, reacts against the presence of Grimes, and Auntie fears things will get out of hand; Ned Keene saves the situation by starting off a round, 'Old Joe has gone fishing', whose 7/4 metre allows for three distinct tunes to be pitted against each other, Grimes's entry almost fatally disrupting the music. Storm music accompanies the arrival of Carter Hobson, Ellen and the new apprentice, chilled to the bone. Auntie offers refreshment, but Grimes wants to be off and takes the boy with him.

Act II. We have seen Grimes as outsider, rebel, dreamer and poet, but in the second act we are to meet him with the two extremes of his character, introspection and violence, very much to the fore. The introductory interlude has a lively *toccata* which contrasts with a broad, appealing lyrical tune, heard first on strings and sung at the rise of the curtain by Ellen, who brings with her John, the new apprentice. The music's mood is at first soft and reflective, as the Borough goes about its Sunday morning business. Ellen's scenes with the boy and later with Grimes take place within a frame provided by the music of the church service, which seems to mirror the moods of the two conversations. During the hymn, Ellen talks to the boy about his life at the workhouse and hers as a teacher and tells him she is determined his new life will be an improvement on the old. As she notices his torn coat and the bruise on this neck, the Confession comes from the church. With the Gloria, she tries to comfort herself and the boy, but the advent of Grimes coincides with the Benedicite and, in spite of Ellen's reminder that it is a day of rest, Grimes orders the boy off to work. Before the Creed begins, Ellen pleads with Peter to be more compassionate, but her music, which is brimming with understanding and tenderness ('Were we mistaken . . .?'), despairingly ends! 'Peter! We've failed', which causes him to cry out in protest and to strike her, matching the chorus's 'Amen' with his own *fortissimo* 'So be it, and God have mercy upon me!'.

Ellen moves aside in tears, but Auntie, Bob Boles and Ned Keene sing a brisk trio based musically on Grimes's cadence: 'Grimes is at his exercise'. The congregation comes out of church on to the beach, half aware of the quarrel taking place outside, and they comment in their different ways – Balstrode urging calm, Swallow sitting on the fence, Bob Boles stirring and demanding to hear from Ellen what was going on. She is inextricably associated in the popular view with Grimes and nothing she says can help the situation, so that the ensemble reaches a climax with a cry of 'Murder!'. The Rector and Swallow feel it encumbent on them to head an investigating party, Carter Hobson beats a call to action which has a sinister ring to it and it is to the sound of a purposeful and vindictive chorus that they march off.

Before the interlude comes a moment of stasis and contemplation as two flutes in seconds introduce a 'trio' for the two Nieces, Auntie and Ellen (except in the first and last phrases the Nieces sing in unison). After the violent action, his calm conclusion is of extraordinary beauty.

The interlude is a *passacaglia*, the centre-piece of the whole opera and built up on Grimes's 'God have mercy upon me'. A desolate solo viola represents the fate of the apprentice caught up in Grimes's destiny. The scene is set in Grimes's hut, an upturned boat full of ropes and tackle. He and the boy come in and prepare to go fishing, as Grimes in a great monologue muses half to himself, half to the boy on the contrast of what he is with what he, with Ellen's help, would like to be. The music is florid and lyrical, until Grimes once again starts a feverish description of his vigil with the dying apprentice in his boat. The sound of the lynch mob can be heard coming nearer. With an admonition to be careful, Grimes hustles the boy down to the boat, only to hear the boy's scream as he falls down the cliff to his death. Grimes scrambles down to see what he can do, but the air is filled with the scream's eerie echo on the celesta. The Rector, Swallow, Keene and Balstrode look into the hut and find order, but comment on the swinging door. Swallow thinks the whole episode may have quietened village gossip once and for all.

Act III. A moon-lit prelude of transparency and beauty introduces the same scene as the first of Act I, the Borough's street and beach. A dance is on at the Moot Hall and bouncy tunes come from off-stage, while the two Nieces contrive to elude the attentions of a rather drunk Swallow. Ned Keene takes his place, when Mrs Sedley tries to enlist his interest in proving Grimes a murderer. A beautiful 'good night' ensemble ensues, the Rector outdoing everyone in affability, but Mrs Sedley broods in the darkness: 'Crime which my hobby is/sweetens my thinking'. She watches Ellen and Balstrode walk up from the beach, the latter revealing that Grimes's boat is in but he nowhere to be found, the former overcome by recognising the boy's jersey found washed up by the tide. Ellen's aria, 'Embroidery in childhood was a luxury of idleness', is the counterpart of Grimes's *scena* in the hut: the music is decorated and exacting and its effect, for all the scene's tension, one of resignation. Balstrode knows that it is the moment of crisis, but thinks there is still something they can do. Mrs Sedley, by contrast, now has the clue she needs and calls officiously for Swallow. Eventually, Hobson

Peter Grimes (Jon Vickers) and the apprentice in Act II (Covent Garden).

summons the men to take a posse to look for Grimes and in an atmosphere of hysteria and brutality the inhabitants of the Borough set out on a man-hunt: 'Him who despises us we'll destroy'. The scene ends with *fortissimo* shouts of 'Peter Grimes', which memorably raised the roof at Sadler's Wells on the first night in 1945.

The last interlude takes us from the crowd's uncontrolled violence to the disintegration of Grimes's mind. When the curtain rises, the search-party's cries can be heard in the distance and at the same time a fog-horn. These sounds form the background to Grimes's long mad scene, virtually unaccompanied, as he babbles of home and sings snatches that remind him of his own tragedy. Ellen and Balstrode tell him they have come to take him home, but it is a moment before he recognises them and when he does it is to the comforting interval of the major ninth. Balstrode instructs him to take his boat out to sea and sink her there, then leads Ellen away.

As the stragglers return from the fruitless chase, the music of the interlude which introduced Act I is heard again: the villagers sing their morning tune and Swallow looks out to sea to confirm the coastguard's report that a sinking boat has been observed. No-one is interested and the Borough seems to be getting on with another day.

Glossary

Bel canto   Literally, the art of singing beautifully; practically, the evolved method of sustaining a vocal line with unshakeable grace and a maximum of expression.

Buffo   Comic. Associated with singers of comic roles or with comic operas, e.g. *Il barbiere di Siviglia.*

Cabaletta   Literally, *cavatinetta*, or a little *cavatina* or song. In practice used to describe the quick final vocal section which sets off and contrasts with a slower aria.

Camerata   A group of Florentine intellectuals who banded together to restore in 16th century Italy the practice of the ancient Greek dramatists, whereby everything was set to music, and music was the servant of the drama.

Cantilena   Used to indicate a slow, unbroken vocal line, often (but not invariably) in connection with an aria.

Coloratura   Literally, coloured, painted. Used in connection with rapid, brilliant singing, often *staccato* (sharply struck detached notes). Properly applied to singing by any vocal range, but in the 20th century often used loosely and illogically to signify light, brilliant sopranos.

Crescendo   A gradual increase in musical volume.

Dodecaphonic   A system pioneered by Schoenberg by which all twelve semi-tones of the chromatic scale were considered of equal importance. From it flowed a new outlook on 'tonality', hitherto the basis of composition, and dodecaphonic music was in no specific key.

Dramma giocoso   A light and lively drama (*giocoso*: playful).

Dramma per musica   Drama *through* music.

Fugato   A combination of a musical theme with itself, the second and third entries beginning half a bar or a bar later and combining to make a musical structure (*Fugato*: literally, pursuing).

Intermezzo   A musical interlude often joining two scenes, sometimes starting an act; usually for orchestra alone.

Legato   Literally, joined. Used to signify a smooth joining of notes or a smooth joining of whole phrases.

Libretto   The 'book' (literally, little book) of an opera.

Ottocento   The Italians used the expression to describe the period 1800 to 1899, which in English would be called the 19th century. Operas of the *ottocento* usually signify Rossini, Donizetti, Bellini and early Verdi.

Passacaglia   A slow dance form built on a fixed bass line. Above it, composers varied the initial tune and in operas, not least of the 20th century (e.g. *Wozzeck, Peter Grimes*), a considerable and often climactic structure could be raised.

Piedigrotta   A Neapolitan Festival of Song, at which until mid-20th century new songs in a traditional style were introduced.

Recitativo secco   Literally, dry recitative. Used to denote the fast sung sentences used to advance the plot between orchestrally accompanied numbers. *Recitativo secco* is accompanied by a single instrument, not by orchestra.

Scena   An expression much used in 19th-century Italian opera to denote a scene in which the action is developed with one or more characters assisting a principal, who usually finishes the *scena* with an aria.

Serialist   Schoenberg's break with tonality was initially often called the Twelve Note system, then dodecaphonic, and eventually his post-1945 followers were described as serialist. The description suggests (but does not insist on) a development of the original system.

Singspiel   German operas of the late 18th and early 19th century often had spoken dialogue between the solo or ensemble numbers. The numbers were usually of a relatively simple nature and it is rare that something so complicated as *Fidelio* or *The Magic Flute* was composed under this discipline.

Spinto   Literally 'squeezed', and is used when a lyrical soprano or tenor evolves more force through what was once thought of as squeezing the voice, and is thus able to tackle heftier roles.

Stretta   The quick section, often finale, which follows a slower movement in Italian opera. It is for more than one voice and often forms the end of a scene.

Tenore di Grazia   A tenor whose method leans more towards the graceful than the forceful; often heard in operas by Rossini.

Terzetto/Trio   A vocal movement for three voices.

Tessitura   Literally, texture. Used to indicate the average height at which a vocal line for a particular role is written. A high or low *tessitura* implies a particular kind of voice, or else an element of strain on a voice which does not live naturally at this level.

Tonality   A structure based on the major and minor scales. After *Tristan*, history suggests that the old system of tonality, on which all classical sonata form was based, had received so great a jolt that it was never the same again. Schoenberg and his followers, according to this reading of history, recognised the jolt and went forward.

Verismo   Literally, realism. Applied to operas whose subjects were concerned with everyday life rather than with history, myth or legend.

Index